Insights into Task-Based Language Teaching

The last few decades have seen an exponential growth in the use of task-based language teaching (TBLT) around the world. Departing from the traditional approaches to language teaching, TBLT offers the opportunity for natural language learning in instructional contexts through the use of authentic and meaning-oriented tasks. This book aims to offer a unique contribution to the expanding literature on TBLT by reflecting current progress in the domain as well as underlining future directions in research and theory. Essential reading for learners, teachers and researchers, the book provides comprehensive coverage on the key elements of TBLT. A fairly wide range of topics such as the rationale for using TBLT, task design, task implementation, and task evaluation is covered in this book. Thus, it is designed to enhance pre-service and practicing teachers' knowledge about TBLT and outline some new directions in which the field should move if it is to fulfill its purposes.

Sima Khezrlou received her PhD in TESOL from Urmia University, Iran. Her research interests include SLA, TBLT, form-focused instruction, and CALL. In addition to a number of publications in these fields, her recent studies include a co-authored article in *System* (2017, with Rod Ellis and Karim Sadeghi) and studies that appear in *RELC, ELT Journal, Journal of Second Language Studies, Language Awareness, The Language Learning Journal, IRAL,* and *Computer Assisted Language Learning.*

Language Teaching Insights Series

Series Editors: David Nunan & Glenn Stockwell

Burston & Arispe: *Mobile-Assisted Language Learning and Advanced-level Second Language Acquisition*

Eginli: *Insights into Emotional Well-Being of Language Teachers*

Farrell: *Insights into Professional Development in Language Teaching*

Horwitz: *Becoming a Language Teacher (2nd ed.)*

Khezrlou: *Insights into Task-Based Language Teaching*

Lai: *Insights into Autonomy and Technology in Language Teaching*

Leis: *Insights into Flipped Classrooms*

Mohebbi (Ed.): *Insights into Teaching and Learning Writing*

Tanaka-Ellis: *Insights into Teaching and Learning with Technology*

More information about titles in this series can be found at
https://www.castledown.com/academic-books/book-series/language-teaching-insights/

Insights into Task-Based Language Teaching

Sima Khezrlou

Melbourne – London – Tokyo – New York

www.castledown.com

4th Floor, Silverstream House, 45 Fitzroy Street Fitzrovia, London W1T 6EB United Kingdom

Level 9, 440 Collins Street, Melbourne, Victoria 3000, Australia

2nd Floor Daiya Building, 2-2-15 Hamamatsu-cho, Minato-ku, Tokyo 105-0013, Japan

447 Broadway, 2nd Floor #393, New York NY, 10013 United States

First published 2022 by Castledown Publishers, London

Information on this title:
www.castledown.com/academic-books/view-title/?reference=9781914291074
DOI: 10.29140/9781914291074

Insights into Task-Based Language Teaching

© Sima Khezrlou, 2022

All rights reserved. This publication is copyright. Subject to statutory exception and to the provisions of relevant collective licencing agreements, no reproduction, transmission, or storage of any part of this publication by any means, electronic, mechanical, photocopying, recording or otherwise may take place without prior written permission from the author.

Typeset by Castledown Design, Melbourne

ISBN: 978-1-914291-07-4 (Paperback)
ISBN: 978-1-914291-08-1 (Digital)

Castledown Publishers takes no responsibility for the accuracy of URLs for external or third-party internet websites referred to in this publication. No responsibility is taken for the accuracy or appropriateness of information found in any of these websites.

Contents

Acknowledgements   xi

PART I   BACKGROUND   1

1 Introduction to Task-Based Language Teaching   3

Introduction   3
The rationale for TBLT   3
Overview of the book   6
Closing commentary   8

PART II   TASK DESIGN   11

2 Types of Tasks in a Task-Based Course   13

Introduction   13
Definition of task   14
    Task as a piece of work in everyday life   14
    Task as an activity or exercise for language learners   14
    Task as an outcome-oriented teaching unit   14
    Task as a behavioral agenda for research   15
    Task as a behavioral agenda for L2 learning   15
Task types   15
    Target tasks and pedagogical tasks   16
    Input-based and output-based tasks   20
    Focused and unfocused tasks   21
    Other task types   23
Conclusion   28

3 Task Selection   30

Introduction   30
Prabhu's approach: Task selection based on topic   31
Long's approach: Task selection based on needs analysis   32

Robinson's approach: Task selection based on cognitive,
ability and affective needs   35
Ellis's approach: Task selection based on learner goals and
interests   38
Conclusion   40

4 Task Complexity and Task Sequencing   42

Introduction   42
Prabhu's approach   43
Long's approach   45
Ellis's approach   47
Skehan's approach   49
Robinson's approach   51
Conclusion   56

PART III   TASK IMPLEMENTATION   59

5 Explicit Instruction in TBLT   61

Introduction   61
The debate over the role of explicit instruction in TBLT   62
FonF in the pre-task stage   66
FonF in the during-task stage   70
FonF in the post-task stage   73
Ellis's proposal for a modular curriculum   75
Conclusion   76

6 Task Repetition   78

Introduction   78
Why TR?   78
Methodological aspects of task repetition   82
    Type of repetition   82
    Number of repetitions   84
    Interval of repetition   85
TR in speaking and writing   88
Form-focused intervention in TR   90
Conclusion   93

7 Task Planning — 94

Introduction — 94
The nature of planning — 95
Types of planning — 96
    Pre-task planning — 96
    Within-task planning — 100
Planning processes — 102
Training task planning — 104
Conclusion — 106

8 Building on Task Performance — 107

Introduction — 107
Transcription — 108
Task modeling — 109
Reflective learning practice — 112
Corrective feedback — 114
    Types of corrective feedback — 115
    Scope of feedback: Focused vs. unfocused — 118
    Timing of corrective feedback — 120
Conclusion — 122

PART IV   ASSESSMENT — 123

9 Task-based Language Assessment — 125

Introduction — 125
Definition and characteristics of TBLA — 125
Components of TBLA — 127
    Test task design and selection — 127
    Implementation of test task — 129
    Performance measurement — 131
Uses of TBLA — 132
Moving forward — 134
Conclusion — 136

PART V: CONCLUSION — 137

10 Conclusion — 139

Introduction — 139
Task design and task implementation — 139
Contextual adaptations to TBLT — 141
Assessment and TBLT — 142
Concluding thoughts — 144

References — *146*

Index — *180*

List of Tables

Table 2.1. Definitions of task as language learning goals — 16

Table 2.2. Definitions of task as an educational activity — 17

Table 4.1. Ellis's criteria for sequencing tasks (Ellis, 2003, pp. 217-228) — 48

Table 5.1. The place of explicit instruction in the TBLT framework — 62

List of Figures

Figure 4.1. Prabhu's task complexity criteria (1987, p. 47)   44

Figure 4.2. Resource-directing versus resource-dispersing dimensions of cognitive task complexity (Robinson, 2000)   53

Acknowledgements

I would like to give a heartfelt thank you to the series editors, David Nunan and Glenn Stockwell, for inviting me to write this book and for their generous encouragement and enthusiasm for this project from its earliest days through its completion. Their expertise and insightful advice were invaluable in developing my thinking and bringing the book together. Thanks also to the editorial team at Castledown Publishers for their amazing support.

As an English language teacher and researcher, the impact of past and present students and colleagues as well as my professors on my thinking and practice has been immense. Among the many people whose ideas I have drawn upon in this book and in my career more generally, Rod Ellis has particularly inspired and shaped my ideas about TBLT. I am forever grateful to you, Rod Ellis, for your inspirational vision.

I dedicate this book to myself and every little dreamer in the whole world who has a dream so big and so exciting. Believe in your dreams and do whatever it takes to achieve them—the best is yet to come for you!

Sima Khezrlou

PART I

BACKGROUND

1
Introduction to Task-Based Language Teaching

Introduction

This introductory chapter lays out the definition, context, and rationale for TBLT. Against this backdrop, I provide a preview of the structure and contents of the book. All chapters of this book cover both pedagogic and research perspectives that inform the design, implementation, and assessment of task-based courses.

The rationale for TBLT

TBLT is an educational framework for the theory and practice of teaching second and foreign languages, which places meaning-based, communicative tasks at the center of language procedures in the classroom (Van den Branden *et al.*, 2009). Distinct from the traditional approaches to language teaching, TBLT regards language as a tool for meaning-making rather than as an object to study (Ellis, 2003). This book offers a lively overview of the current developments in the field of TBLT, and provides researchers, learners and language practitioners with both the theoretical insights and practical means required to understand and research key elements of TBLT. A fairly wide range of topics such as task design, task implementation, and task-based assessment is covered in this book.

Task-based language teaching is a broadly defined approach to language teaching research and practice that is based on the use of "task" as its core unit. The term task has emerged from a body of research that views communicative interaction as substantial to language learning. TBLT has been grounded within experiential "learning by doing" educational philosophy espoused by Dewey and others (Long, 2015; Samuda & Bygate, 2008). The rationale for TBLT as a teaching approach is rooted in theories of language acquisition that stress the effect of meaningful language use together with opportunities to notice the target language on language learning (e.g., Long, 1996; Skehan, 1998). Based on such theories, opportunities for communicative language use and noticing form-meaning mappings provide the conditions under which communicative competence in a second language (L2) can most effectively be developed (Willis & Willis, 2007). Translated into classroom practice, TBLT is materialized as weak and strong versions. The weak version, or what Ellis (2003) refers to as "task-supported language teaching," uses tasks in addition to another unit, such as linguistic forms, functions, skills, lexis, or concepts. The strong version, regarded by Ellis as "task-based language teaching," on the other hand, uses "task" as the only unit of analysis for syllabus design. The tendency for teachers to adapt TBLT into their instructional contexts in the form of task-supported language teaching is a topic addressed in a number of sections in this book.

Over the past three decades, TBLT has attracted the interest of second language acquisition (SLA) researchers, curriculum developers, teacher trainers, teachers, and practitioners. This is evidenced by abundant journal articles including special issues in prominent journals, symposiums, seminars, colloquiums, academic sessions, and conference presentations. Indeed, the International Consortium on Task-based Language Teaching (ICTBLT) was formed in 2005 which holds a biennial international conference on the topic, now transformed into a professional association, named International Association for Task-Based Language Teaching (IATBLT). More recently, a new journal has been specifically dedicated to the topic, *TASK: Journal on Task-Based Language Teaching and Learning*, the first volume of which appeared in 2021. There is also a dedicated book series on topics in TBLT published by John Benjamins. The persistently rising popularity of TBLT as an approach to language teaching may be ascribed to its emphasis on meaning-making and engagement with real-world language needs. TBLT is based on the use of tasks, typically selected by the authentic needs of the learners, and the resulting linguistic forms, as the basis of language curricula, syllabi, instruction, and assessment (Long, 2015). The approach is notably different from the traditional language teaching, which is centered on discrete grammatical forms, vocabulary, or structures, and generally instructed in the order prescribed by a textbook. In recent years, educators and governments around the world have moved progressively towards different versions of TBLT as a potential solution for curricula that do not bring about authentic and meaningful engagement with L2 learning and fail to effectively motivate learners as a result. Thus, no wonder many teachers around the world are switching their pedagogy toward TBLT in accordance with the strong belief that TBLT enhances SLA and makes L2 learning and teaching more fruitful and more rewarding. In fact, it is now well-established that TBLT represents an innovative approach to L2 learning and teaching at both theoretical and methodological levels. Theoretically, TBLT perceives SLA as a process not directly impacted by formal instruction, but which is cultivated through the meaningful use of language. And methodologically, TBLT views learners as language users rather than learners, with the explicit examination of linguistic features and structures arising from difficulties experienced during the performance of tasks (Bygate, 2016; Long, 2015).

Prior research in TBLT has been mainly rooted in cognitive-interactionist and pedagogical traditions that are interested in exploring how tasks relate to cognitive variables, how they lead to varied language production, and how they are designed and implemented in authentic classroom contexts. These paradigms constitute the most fruitful, yet most disputed, areas of research in TBLT and, as a result, deserve more attention in order to move the field forward. A number of areas where our knowledge about TBLT is still limited include: (a) how and which task features give rise to more effective interaction and L2 acquisition particularly in the long run, (b) how the task design features and task implementation conditions can be effectively manipulated to suit learners with different levels of linguistic capabilities, (c) how the TBLT curricula can be implemented or adapted in different instructional contexts, and (d) how task-based language assessment (TBLA) can be effectively designed, organized, and implemented to help enhance student learning and motivation. In keeping with these central themes, the subsequent chapters' focus will provide accounts of a range of approaches to task design, task implementation, and task-based language assessment that are of relevance to practitioners and researchers alike.

Overview of the book

This book is broken into five parts: background, design, implementation, and assessment. This introductory chapter served to present background information on TBLT. The second part of the book describes the various design elements in TBLT. Chapter 2 reviews different approaches to the definition of task. In the past two decades, tasks have been defined in a variety of ways. Nevertheless, although characteristics of language tasks have been summarized in different ways in the TBLT literature, there is a lot of common ground shared in these definitions which are all illuminated in this chapter. Chapter 2 further describes different task types including target tasks and pedagogical tasks, input-based and output-based tasks, focused and unfocused tasks, open and closed tasks, one-way and two-way tasks, convergent and divergent tasks, and monologic and dialogic tasks. Chapter 3 overviews the pedagogical components—how the tasks are selected and situated in task-based lessons based on different frameworks. The approach presented by Long (1985, 2015), building on a needs analysis, underscores the importance of learners' ability to enact tasks that are likely to be faced by learners in the real-world. And, whereas Robinson's (2011a) approach to task-based syllabus design requires the specification of the cognitive and affective demands of tasks, Ellis (2018) adopts a similar approach as Prabhu (1987) in underlining the role of teachers in selecting tasks based on their knowledge of their learners. The last chapter in Part II is related to task complexity and task sequencing. Chapter 4 reviews the early TBLT proposals that specify several factors that impact the complexity of a task as well as the theories of task complexity and the research they have produced on the issue of grading tasks. This chapter offers recommendations for teachers to have an idea about the complexity of a specific task and to determine its suitability for their groups of learners based on a list of variables that can help them sharpen their intuitions.

Part III of the book turns towards the task implementation variables which are argued to be more likely to exert a much greater effect on task performance than design variables and be of greater importance for achieving a balanced and effective L2 learning (Skehan, 2016). Part III includes critical discussion and reviews empirical studies that discuss foundational constructs related to task-based performance and pedagogy such as the role of explicit instruction in TBLT, task repetition, task planning, and post-task focus on form strategies. Chapter 5 opens this Part by describing the role of explicit instruction in TBLT—how form-focused instruction is situated at different parts of the TBLT cycle: pre-task, during-task, and post-task. This chapter also presents Ellis's (2018) proposal for a modular curriculum that combines TBLT and traditional approaches in case the implementation of TBLT becomes difficult in some educational contexts. Chapter 6 is a review of task repetition, a prominent task implementation option in the TBLT literature. This chapter addresses the theoretical basis for repetition research, namely Skehan's limited attention capacity model or trade-off hypothesis, and Levelt's speech production model. The chapter further attends to key methodological issues in task repetition research such as type of repetition, number of repetitions, and interval of repetition. Other topics that have been more recently attended to in the task repetition literature and are covered in Chapter 6 include the comparative effectiveness of repeated performances in L2 speaking versus writing tasks as well as the role of form-focused intervention between repeated task performances to reinforce the focus on form potential of task repetition. In Chapter 7, the nature of task planning, types of planning, and the importance of planning processes are discussed as a precursor to a review of studies in each section. Within the task planning literature there is a dearth of research on what actually happens when learners plan for the task. Thus, to understand better why and how task planning can enhance output, it is necessary to look into how learners behave during their planning time, and what strategies they employ to help them address the task demands in language that is accurate, fluent and suitably complex. These issues are also dealt with in Chapter 7. This chapter concludes by emphasizing the role that training learners to use effective pre-task planning strategies plays in transferring the planned speech/writing to the actual task performance. Part III ends with Chapter 8 which presents an overview of the utilization of post-task activities with a focus on form function. Numerous activities such as transcription, task modeling, reflection, and corrective feedback which are argued to promote attention and consolidation of linguistic structures are included in this chapter.

Task-based language assessment (TBLA) is the focus of Part IV. TBLA is an approach to language assessment that focuses on what learners can do with language in contrast to what they know about language (Van Gorp & Deygers, 2013). It, thus, stands in contrast with what is described as a test or instrument administered as an evaluator rather than an enabler of student learning. Through focusing on how TBLA can be effectively implemented by clarifying its purpose, characteristics, and components as well as the measurement of assessment outcomes, this chapter aims at providing teachers with guidance to implement TBLA as a practice to transform their traditional approach into effective language pedagogy. However, in spite of the pedagogic benefits associated with the task-based approach to assessment, it remains a domain that faces several challenges in its implementation. The remainder of Chapter 9 discusses how adopting formative assessment in TBLT and the provision of necessary training for teachers can crucially affect the practice of TBLA in the classroom. Lastly, Part V encompasses the concluding chapter (Chapter 10) which summarizes the main insights obtained in the book and articulates new directions for further discussion and exploration.

Closing commentary

As noted at the outset, the current book pursued the aim of providing theoretical and methodological accounts for the place of TBLT in language education and presenting cutting-edge empirical research that can help advance research agendas. Hence, the book is intended as a contribution to theory and research on TBLT and L2 pedagogy and one of its unique features is that it integrates in-depth theoretical and methodological reflections with most recent areas of empirical research and findings in a single book. In the Conclusion chapter (Chapter 10), I evaluate the contribution of the book with respect to what it adds to prior theoretical and empirical initiatives, and what directions for future inquiry it opens up. The Conclusion chapter will be the finale of a journey that I now invite readers to commence. It is hoped that through this journey readers interpret the concoction of directions and methodologies in the empirical research, along with the exhaustive theoretical and methodological considerations entailed in the book, as evidence of the TBLT's significant contributions to advancing understandings of pedagogy and language learning.

PART II

TASK DESIGN

2
Types of Tasks in a Task-Based Course

Introduction

Task-based language teaching uses task, in contrast to language, as the instructional unit in language classrooms (Long, 2015). Whereas the traditional synthetic syllabuses present language in discrete grammatical units, demanding learners to synthesize forms to develop meaning when required to do so, TBLT underscores authentic, communication-oriented tasks that offer task-related focus on form in line with a learner's own internal syllabus (Bryfonski & McKay, 2019). The purpose of TBLT is to prepare learners to utilize their linguistic skills in meaningful interactions outside the classroom. To achieve this purpose, TBLT uses tasks, typically based on the authentic needs of the learners, and the resultant language forms, as the basis of language curricula, syllabi, teaching, and assessment (Long, 2015). Nevertheless, the idea of task may not be as simple as it might seem. There are numerous definitions and viewpoints about what constitutes a task. In L2 teaching and learning, task is commonly perceived as an outcome-oriented teaching unit or as a behavioral structure for research or classroom learning. Most often, the definition of task may differ based on different task purposes. In this chapter, I first present the definitions of and perspectives on the idea of task followed by general and specific typologies of tasks used for both research and teaching purposes.

Definition of task

Task as a piece of work in everyday life

According to Long (1985), a task is "... a piece of work undertaken for oneself or for others, freely or for some reward . . . [B]y 'task' is meant the hundred and one things people do in everyday life, at work, at play, and in between" (p. 89). The distinctive emphasis in Long's definition is related to the real-world relationship for an activity to qualify as a task.

Task as an activity or exercise for language learners

In fact, there are several activities or exercises in different types of L2 textbooks that learners need to accomplish. These activities or exercises are generally termed as tasks although they do not have a specific focus on outcome.

Task as an outcome-oriented teaching unit

Similar to task as an activity or exercise, this definition considers task as an activity for L2 learners to complete, yet it also emphasizes an outcome that the L2 learner is expected to produce or achieve. Accordingly, the task is an outcome-oriented unit of teaching in a curriculum or lesson plan. This concept stems from adult vocational education which was later expanded to elementary education and other areas, such as L2 learning and teaching (Richards & Rodgers, 2001). Likewise, Breen (1987) considers a language task as a structured language effort that is based on a particular goal, proper content, a specific procedure, and several possible outcomes for those who perform it. Breen argued that language tasks can be considered as an array of work plans, ranging from simple to complex, with the general objective of enhancing L2 learning. Indeed, according to Breen, "all materials for language teaching . . . can be seen as compendia of tasks" (Breen, 1987, p. 26). Similarly, Prabhu contended that a task "is an activity that requires learners to arrive at an outcome from given information through some process of thought, and which allows teachers to control and regulate that process" (1987, p. 17). Based on these definitions, then, a task is viewed as a structured teaching blueprint that demands learners to approach a goal or outcome using specific performance procedures usually provided by the teachers. And, in this definition, the task is imposed from the outside and does not come from the learner.

Task as a behavioral agenda for research

Activity Theory, rooted in the work of Vygotsky (1978) and his colleagues, poses a substantial question: "What is the individual or group doing in a particular setting?" (Wertsch, 1985, p. 211). Coughlin and Duff (1994, p. 175), following Activity Theory, differentiated between an L2 task and an L2 activity. Based on this definition, a task alludes to the "behavioral blueprint provided to students in order to elicit data" for research or assessment. Activity, on the other hand, was defined by Coughlin and Duff as "the behavior that is actually produced when an individual (or group) performs a task" (1994, p. 175). This difference can be important when a task is assumed to stimulate diverse activities across individuals and in the same individual on distinct occasions.

Task as a behavioral agenda for L2 learning

In teaching contexts, drawing on Vygotskian concepts, a task entails the instructions or guidance provided by the teacher to the learners for the purpose of learning—that is, the behavioral blueprint presented to students in order to achieve learning. And, an activity refers to the learners' actual performance using these instructions, that is, the behavior irrespective of whether it is observable or entirely cognitive that takes place when learners enact a task that has been presented to them.

Task types

The TBLT literature encompasses a wide range of suggestions for distinguishing different types of tasks, leaving no clear-cut, agreed-upon way of classifying tasks. By and large, pedagogical accounts have attempted to differentiate tasks with respect to the operations learners are asked to go through when they carry out them. Below, different classifications for task types based on the features of tasks are presented.

Target tasks and pedagogical tasks

Nunan (1989) makes a distinction between target tasks and pedagogical tasks. To Nunan, the former indicates the language use in the world beyond classrooms—also termed as real-world tasks—while the latter takes place in classrooms. Brown (2007) makes a similar distinction as Nunan. He stresses that TBLT draws a significant difference between target tasks that learners are expected to attain beyond the classroom, and pedagogical tasks, which form the nucleus of the classroom activities. Table 2.1 demonstrates the definitions of tasks where the target task is regarded as central.

Table 2.1 *Definitions of task as language learning goals*

Scholar	Definition
Long (1985, p. 89)	"A piece of work undertaken for oneself or for others, freely or for some reward. Thus, examples of tasks include painting a fence, dressing a child, filling out a form, and helping someone across a road. In other words, by 'task' is meant the hundred and one things people do in everyday life, at work, at play, and in between".
Carroll (1993)	Any activity in which a person engages, given an appropriate setting, in order to achieve a specifiable class of objectives.
Bachman and Palmer (1996, p. 44)	"An activity that involves individuals in using language for the purpose of achieving a particular goal or objective in a particular situation".

The definitions presented in Table 2.1 all suggest that tasks are activities individuals do, which consist of the active participation of language users. Tasks are context-specific in life and they are purpose-oriented. According to Long's definition, we can see that, even though the purpose of the learner in enacting a task is not related to language, the task may include language use for its completion. For example, filling out a form seems to be non-linguistic, yet it becomes a language task if it cannot be performed without language use, such as understanding the instructions from others. The definition provided by Bachman and Palmer signifies that language use is a means to an end. In other words, by understanding language input, by producing language output, by interacting with other individuals in real-life contexts through the use of language, the objectives that the learner has in mind can be better accomplished (Branden, 2006).

Successful implantation of TBLT in the classroom context is dependent on the use of pedagogical tasks. Table 2.2 presents a list of definitions describing some significant features of task as an educational activity.

Table 2.2 *Definitions of task as an educational activity*

Scholar	Definition
Richards, Platt and Weber (1985, p. 289)	"An activity or action which is carried out as the result of processing or understanding language (i.e. as a response). For example, drawing a map while listening to a tape, listening to an instruction and performing a command may be referred to as tasks. Tasks may or may not involve the production of language. A task usually requires the teacher to specify what will be regarded as a successful completion of the task. The use of a variety of different kinds of tasks in language teaching is said to make language teaching more communicative… since it provides a purpose for a classroom activity which goes beyond the practice of language for its own sake."
Breen (1987, p. 23)	"Any structured language learning endeavor which has a particular objective, appropriate content, a specified working procedure, and a range of outcomes for those who undertake the task. 'Task' is therefore assumed to refer to a range of work plans which have the overall purposes of facilitating language learning from the simple and brief exercise type, to more complex and lengthy activities such as group problem-solving or simulations and decision-making."

Prabhu (1987, p. 24)	"An activity which required learners to arrive at an outcome from given information through some process of thought and which allowed teachers to control and regulate that process was regarded as a task."
Candlin (1987, p. 10)	"One of a set of differentiated, sequenceable, problem-posing activities involving learners' cognitive and communicative procedures applied to existing and new knowledge in the collective exploration and pursuance of foreseen or emergent goals within a social milieu."
Willis (1996, p. 23)	"Activities where the target language is used by the learner for a communicative purpose (goal) in order to achieve an outcome."
Ur (1996, pp. 123–124)	"A task is essentially goal-oriented; it requires the group or pair to achieve an objective that is usually expressed by an observable result, such as brief notes or lists, a spoken summary. This result should be attainable only by the interaction between participants."
Skehan (1998, p. 95)	"An activity in which: - Meaning is primary; - There is some communication problem to solve; - There is some sort of relationship to comparable real-world - activities; - Task completion has some priority; - The assessment of the task is in terms of outcome; - Tasks do not give other people's meaning to regurgitate; - Tasks are not concerned with language display; - Tasks are not conformity-oriented; - Tasks are not practice-oriented; - Tasks do not embed language into materials so that specific structures can be focused upon."
Ellis (2003, pp. 9–10)	- A task is a workplan; - A task involves a primary focus on meaning; - A task involves real-world processes of language use;

	- A task can involve any of the four language skills; - A task engages cognitive processes; - A task has a clearly defined communicative outcome.

The definitions in Table 2.2 underscore the crucial role of meaning, illuminating that the learners' focus should be on the exchange or negotiation of meaning through completing tasks. These definitions, in fact, imply that the purpose of pedagogical tasks is that they need to facilitate meaningful interaction and provide the learner abundant opportunities to analyze meaningful input and produce output in order to attain relevant and achievable goals (Carless, 2003). In other words, through performing tasks, learners function as a language user rather than a language learner, and a learner's performance on pedagogical tasks acts as a means for them to behave communicatively, such as natural negotiation of meaning. A close connection needs to be created between the tasks performed in the classroom and those done in the outside world; a pedagogical task as a piece of classroom work needs to imitate activities that the learners may perform in daily life, thereby reproducing processes of everyday communication. To put it differently, the pedagogical tasks learners do in the classroom should remind learners of what they will do in the real world using the media of the target language. That is, tasks need to be authentic language activities.

Nonetheless, to what extent the pedagogical tasks need to resemble target tasks is a question deserving to be explored further. None of the definitions in the above table clarifies unambiguously the exact link between target tasks and pedagogical tasks. It is noted easily that, even though some tasks implemented in the classroom are genuine copies of target tasks, there are several other ones which cannot set up a real-world context for learners, such as spotting the differences in two pictures. However, Ellis (2003) explains that such tasks can be said to depict some type of relationship with the real world since the kind of language behavior they stimulate is correspondent to the communicative behavior required when carrying out real-world tasks. The authenticity of pedagogical tasks may be relative, in that tasks can be like the real-world tasks or found only in class, but, whatever tasks are used, they should provide learners with opportunities to communicate freely.

Input-based and output-based tasks

A task can be input-based, asking learners to basically process the oral or written information presented and indicate their comprehension of it (for instance by drawing a picture or making a model), or it can be output-based, requiring the learners to write or speak in order to accomplish the task outcome. This difference is crucial since, as Prabhu (1987) underlined, learners at lower levels of proficiency cannot be expected to use the L2 productively; thus, TBLT must be input-driven in the beginning. An input-based task is normally developed following two goals: a) to engage learners in input comprehension, and b) to direct learners' attention to particular linguistic forms in a meaningful context. In fact, recent research particularly through the use of eye-tracking method has verified learners' longer fixations for new words than known words in written input (Godfroid *et al.*, 2018; Pellicer-Sánchez, 2016; Puimège *et al.*, 2021), and focused on both grammatical forms (e.g., Benati, 2021; Lee & Révész, 2020) and phonological forms in terms of syllable-tone combinations (Wiener *et al.*, 2021). One of the most common types of input-based tasks is listen-and-do task where learners have to listen to verbal input and show their comprehension of target language non-verbally, for example by selecting the accurate picture about the target L2 forms between two options. It is presumed that this type of task enables learners to naturally focus on the target L2 forms in order to complete the task. Considering that production is not forbidden, learners are free to be involved in interaction with the teacher and learn the target linguistic forms from the interaction.

The development of the Output Hypothesis and Swain's (1998, 2005) arguments that output does not just present opportunities for language use but might also help SLA promote the prominence of output-based tasks in the classroom. According to Swain, output facilitates SLA through promoting noticing, providing opportunities for learners to test hypotheses about how the target language works, and opportunities for reflection on learners' own language productions. A large number of studies have tested these assumptions and verified the noticing role of output in helping L2 learners become aware of the gaps in their existing interlanguage and the target language they need to learn in order to express their ideas (e.g., Izumi, 2002; Izumi & Bigalow, 2000; Swain & Lapkin, 1995; Zalbidea, 2021). During the performance of output-based tasks, learners' awareness would be naturally drawn to the problems in their interlanguage capabilities; hence, they might pay close attention to linguistic forms in the subsequent input, if any, to fill their gaps. A recent study by Duong, Perez, Desmet and Peters (2021) highlighted the usefulness of completing both input-based and output-based speaking tasks rather than a mere exposure to input-only with no subsequent task in learning words. Nevertheless, these results are limited to L2 vocabulary acquisition, and more research needs to be conducted on other linguistic forms to verify (or disprove) these effects.

Focused and unfocused tasks

Tasks can also vary regarding whether they fall within or outside the focus on form approach which aims "to elicit the use of specific linguistic features in the context of meaning-centered language use" (Ellis *et al.*, 2002, p. 420). The term "form" in this definition concerns the formal linguistic aspects such as phonology, vocabulary, grammar, or pragmatics (Ellis, 2009a). When a task is focused, the form is typically pre-specified. Therefore, focused tasks are categorized as a type of "planned focus on form" (Ellis *et al.*, 2002). In this task type, learners are required to use a particular grammar form to complete the task. For instance, consider a task that asks learners to play the role of a shopkeeper. Learners don't have access to their partner's information, but they have to persuade them that one particular smartphone is better than another. The expected situation is that learners would end up making use of comparative structures to complete the task. Focused tasks should be designed in such a way that learners attend to meaningful issues (such as selling a phone they want to sell), yet at the same time have to employ particular linguistic forms, such as the comparative structures required in this example. Another type of focused task which can be used in the language classroom is text reconstruction. In this task, learners encounter linguistic features that occur frequently in the target text, based on which they are asked to underline the parts that they find most important for subsequent reconstruction. Consciousness-raising task is another type of focused task that explicitly requires a focus on linguistic form. In this task type, the teacher can opt for a feature that poses challenges for learners to acquire. One might think of the past-counterfactual conditional structure in English as a case in point. By making this structure the focus of the task, the teacher would be able to ensure that learners pay attention to that feature, yet, at the same time, they can exchange their views and have a meaningful interaction on a language feature. Consciousness-raising tasks have been shown to be valuable in effectively attracting learners' attention to difficult structures and resulting in not just conscious knowledge of a target structure but also its automatization through subsequent practice opportunities (see Khezrlou, 2022). In contrast to the focused tasks, in unfocused tasks, learners exchange meaning with no specific grammatical feature being needed to complete the task. Therefore, these tasks do not have the particular goal of prompting the use of particular grammatical features in learners' productions. One example would be a simple storytelling task where a learner builds up a story based on a series of picture prompts. Narrative tasks are a well-established and frequently researched task type in the TBLT literature (Bygate, 1999; Foster & Skehan, 1996).

Both focused and unfocused tasks are valuable in that they present opportunities for L2 learners to use the target language meaningfully, yet only the former are developed with the purpose of obtaining particular linguistic forms in the learners' output. Nonetheless, what both task types share is their main purpose to promote communicative language use. As Loshky and Bley-Vroman (1993) have put, focused tasks can be designed in a way to stimulate the natural arousal of a target linguistic structure in the learner's production, or to become useful for the completion of the task, or, finally, must be used if the learner aims at completing the task. Although Loshky and Bley-Vroman mentioned the challenges in designing tasks that elicit a linguistic feature vital for task completion, numerous research studies published over the past two decades have revealed the practicality of developing tasks to draw learners' attention to linguistic features from simple to complex structures (see Loewen & Sato, 2021, for a review). Nevertheless, these studies have also revealed that (1) learners' attention may not always be focused on the features pursued by the teacher or the researcher, (2) some forms are easier to extract compared to others, and (3) producing a form during the performance of a communication-oriented task does not ensure the learning of that feature. In addition, there would be individual variations in the use of a linguistic structure in focused tasks in the classroom.

In sum, then, although the development and use of focused communicative tasks can be challenging for both teachers and researchers, various studies have divulged the role of both focused and unfocused tasks in prompting the use of language-related episodes (Swain, 1998) where learners attend to the language they are using with no teacher intervention to draw attention to linguistic issues (Basterrechea & Leeser, 2019; Qin, 2008; Svalberg & Askham, 2020). In that sense, both focused and unfocused tasks are useful in helping learners attend to form while they engage in the exchange of meaning.

Other task types

There are several other ways of classifying tasks based on the research conducted on the communicative and cognitive processes included in enacting different tasks resulting in a number of features. These various and specific features that a task entails can influence the language the task elicits.

Open versus closed tasks

The first category is related to the open versus closed aspect of the tasks. Nunan (1991) defines an open task as one that does not have a specific correct answer (e.g., opinion gap tasks), and a closed task as one that demands a sole accurate answer or a limited number of correct responses (e.g., spot-the-difference tasks). Long (1989) distinguishes between closed and open tasks in terms of the quantity and quality of negotiation for meaning, which according to him, are much higher on closed tasks. Long explains that "when participants know that task completion depends on their finding the answer, not settling on any answer they choose when the going gets rough and moving on to something else" (p. 45). From this perspective, then, all other things being equal, closed tasks are more likely to obtain language recycling, greater negotiation for meaning, more feedback, more accuracy, and so forth. Contrary to closed tasks, open tasks lead to "free conversation" which makes speakers "treat topics briefly, to drop them altogether when serious trouble arises, to provide feedback to their interlocutors less often, to incorporate feedback from their interlocutors less often, and to recycle linguistic material less often than when the same speakers work together on various other 'problem-solving' tasks" (Long, 1989, p. 44).

The language use and interactional patterns elicited by the open and closed tasks have been subject to some empirical research. Nunan (1991) compared the interactional patterns of L2 English learners in a closed task which asked learners to assign 20 vocabulary cards into semantic fields and an open task which required learners to read a text on habits and engage in an open-ended discussion on bad habits. Nunan found that different task types not only led to diverse interactional patterns, they were also affected by learners' levels of proficiency such that with lower-intermediate to intermediate learners, closed tasks acted better in stimulating more modified interaction than open tasks. These findings, however, should not mean that such learners need to be asked to perform only closed tasks; rather, a variety of tasks that meet the pedagogic objectives of the curriculum need to be used in the classroom. As Harris and Leeming (2020) underline, open and closed tasks exist on a scale rather than constituting a simple dichotomy. Tasks differ in the extent to which they are open or closed. For instance, in a narrative task, whereas pictures may imply a specific story, learners have the freedom to understand them to develop their own original story. Therefore, it is possible to design tasks which predict language use to different extents and use them in different instructional settings and for different learners; however, there is currently limited empirical evidence to support these speculations.

One-way versus two-way tasks

Long (1989) has also made a distinction between one-way and two-way tasks that differ regarding information distribution and are pertinent to the nature of the learners' produced discourse on task. One-way/two-way distinction concerns the way information is distributed and the structure of the task that requires learners to exchange information to complete the task successfully. In other words, in a one-way task, one learner is given all of the task-essential information in order to communicate it to the other(s), as in telling a story. In a two-way task, on the other hand, the task-essential information is distributed between all of the learners who must share and integrate it (Long, 1989), as in an information-gap pair work. Some researchers have shown that it is the two-way tasks that are more conducive of negotiation work. In fact, there is a general consensus among researchers such as Long (1989), Varonis and Gass (1985), Doughty and Pica (1986), Pica (1987), and Pica *et al.* (1993) that when two-way tasks are used in group work and pair work requiring learners to share key information that is preliminarily disseminated only partially to each member, a promising condition is provided for learners to negotiate meaning through the conversational adjustments they make in interaction. Nevertheless, this position in favor of two-way tasks for successful negotiation of meaning is challenged in other studies (Duff, 1986; Nakahama *et al.*, 2001; Slimani-Rolls, 2005), indicating the lack of two-way tasks' supremacy over one-way tasks. Varonis and Gass (1985) and Jauregi (1990) reported that it was, in effect, the one-way task that led to more meaning negotiation. As a result, if the purpose of negotiation studies is to segregate the most helpful task type to bring about language acquisition in the classroom, they have done little, yet signify a reasonable use of a balanced diet of one-way and two-way tasks as currently the safest way for teachers.

Convergent versus divergent tasks

The other task type category is based on the task goal. Task goal is a significant aspect of a task since the eventual aim of getting L2 learners to perform tasks is to obtain a non-linguistic task goal through interaction (Ellis, 2003; Erlam, 2016; Long, 2015; Skehan, 2014). According to Pica *et al.*'s (1993) taxonomy, task goals can be manipulated along the communication goal and are categorized as having either convergent or divergent goals. In convergent tasks, learners need to arrive at a consensus in order to accomplish the task goal. On the other hand, in divergent tasks, learners digress towards the task goal during task performance having numerous outcome options with feasibly more than one goal (Hommel, 2011). Two tasks that represent this task type category are a decision-making task (convergent task) and an opinion-exchange task (divergent task). Previous studies have demonstrated that task goal orientation manipulated along convergent and divergent goals had significant effects on the occurrence of negotiation for meaning and thereby more effective L2 learning (Long, 1996; Mackey, 2012). Tasks with a convergent outcome augmented turn exchanges, fortified learners' engagement in negotiation for meaning (Duff, 1986; Jackson, 2007; Keller-Lally, 2006), and fostered their collaboration when they worked toward a single task goal (Skehan, 2001; Wegerif *et al.*, 1999). Duff (1986) argues that in convergent tasks, learners need to solve a specific problem in pairs in order to arrive at a solution, whereas in divergent tasks, learners should cover a wide array of topics, different perspectives and procedures to endorse a particular position and prove their partner's position false with as many arguments as possible. Duff's study showed that the use of convergent tasks (problem solving) resulted in more negotiation of meaning in comparison to divergent tasks (debating). Based on these findings, he concluded that while convergent tasks led to more comprehensible input, divergent tasks encouraged more output. Similarly, Long (1989) found that convergent tasks were associated with more turns, questions, and confirmation checks per task than divergent tasks. Dao's (2019) findings also suggest that designing tasks with a convergent goal orientation was more effective in enhancing both cognitive engagement in terms of the production of idea units and language related episodes as well as promoting social engagement in terms of responsiveness between learners. Nonetheless, Skehan and Foster (2001) revealed that divergent tasks were more likely to facilitate learners' linguistic productions using more complex syntactic structures compared to convergent tasks. In any case, it would seem more important to develop tasks that encourage meaningful interaction between learners, so the interface between negotiation and task goal seems to be an area of research in need of more attention.

Monologic versus dialogic tasks

The last task type reviewed in this chapter is the monologic versus dialogic task which has not received much attention in TBLT research. As the names suggest, a monologue encompasses the production of sequences by one speaker, while a dialogue is a joint endeavor including more than one individual who take turns to communicate (Cameron, 2001). According to Edwards (2008), what distinguishes a dialogue from a monologue include between-turn pauses, interruptions by the speakers, and concurrent conversation. The collaborative and interactive nature of a dialogue helps the L2 speakers use their partner's turn to plan for their utterances (Webber, 2008). This may imply that having some time to listen facilitates speakers' conceptualization (where the preverbal message is produced) and reformulation (where the preverbal message is changed into a phonetic plan for speech) based on Levelt's (1989) model of speech production. This extra planning time during the interlocutor's turn makes Tavakoli and Foster (2008) suggest that task performance in a dialogic task is cognitively simpler than language processing in a monologic task. Another simplification in dialogic tasks pertains to the interlocutor's role in helping out as soon as the partner becomes silent in an attempt to keep a constant flow of communication (Michel *et al.*, 2012). In contrast, in a monologic task, speakers need to perform all processes of language production concurrently, leading to serial processing of information which may result in hesitations (Levelt, 1989). Thus, in a dialogic task, L2 learners are more likely to interact such that they can benefit from the interactional processes focusing their attention to both form and meaning. On the other hand, one also needs to consider that dialogues may also distract learners' attention from their own performance since partners perform the double role of speaker and listener. As Rost (2011) clarifies, listening and comprehension in interaction is a complicated and demanding task. In contrast, in a monologic task, learners can stay with their own knowledge and resources yet they also have to depend on these. They do not obtain other feedback and no interactional adjustments will attract their focus on neither form nor meaning. The only way to bring about modified output is by monitoring their own speech, an arduous procedure that requires time and attentional capacity particularly in the L2 (Kormos, 2000).

Up to now, a handful of studies have compared the effects of monologic and dialogic tasks in terms of interaction and task performance. Skehan and Foster's (2007) meta-analysis highlighted that dialogues led to greater linguistic accuracy and complexity, but resulted in lower fluency. Nevertheless, this meta-analysis compared L2 performances on several different tasks that manipulated diverse task factors making it hard to arrive at overall conclusions. Tavakoli's (2016) study reported that performance in a dialogic task (a retelling task) was significantly better than a monologic task (a discussion task) in terms of speed, length of pause, and repair measures; however, number and location of pauses were not found to be different in the two modes. In another study, Michel *et al.* (2012) found the consistent superiority of dialogic tasks regarding accuracy, lexical complexity, and fluency. These studies indicate the existence of differences between the monologic and dialogic task performances, signifying the need for more research to provide a better understanding of the factors that encourage a more effective task performance in interactive tasks such as a dialogue versus monologic performances such as story retelling tasks.

Conclusion

In this chapter, I attempted to shed light on how task design features influence the types of interaction that result from a task. Several categories for the task types and the pertinent research in this area were presented in this chapter leading to a number of general conclusions:

- Tasks are context-specific and they are purpose-oriented with language use serving as a means to an end.
- Tasks as a piece of classroom work, namely pedagogical tasks, need to remind learners of what they will do in the real world using the media of the target language.
- Input-based tasks that establish a purposeful need for learners to map forms onto their meanings are effective for L2 learning. And, they work even better when learners have opportunities to interact when they do not understand the input.
- Output tasks particularly when learners have opportunities to repair their errors is also effective in leading to noticing of linguistic forms.
- As long as they provide opportunities for L2 learners to use the target language meaningfully, both focused tasks that require the

use of a particular grammatical feature for task completion and unfocused tasks that do not have such a requirement work for acquisition.
- Tasks can be developed to serve different purposes based on the learning needs and the instructional focus in each classroom context. For example, an information-gap task that asks a learner to give thorough descriptions of a number of pictures so that another learner can spot the items is one-way, monologic, closed, and convergent. An opinion-gap task that gives learners information and asks them to decide to award a scholarship to one of four candidates is two-way, dialogic, open, and divergent.

These conclusions are based on theoretical frameworks and research findings. Yet, considering the scarcity of research and the inconsistency of results in some cases, these points are essentially tentative. Also, as I have noted, the interplay of a number of factors in the design of tasks and the multidimensional purposes that tasks may serve make it hard to arrive at clear-cut conclusions. Therefore, it would be helpful if more research is reported on how and which task features give rise to more effective interaction and L2 acquisition in the long-term. This should give us a more transparent understanding of which task features have a more prominent contribution to make in influencing task performance.

One last point worthy of highlighting here is that the hard-pressed teachers generally have difficulty finding the time (and perhaps the skills) to develop their own materials (Ellis, 2019). This lack of materials has been lamented for a long time. The TBLT Language Learning Task Bank—a new initiative of the International Association for Task-Based Language Teaching (IATBLT)—provides a potential solution where language teachers and researchers can share their tasks as well as how successful those tasks turn out to be in a particular context. This bank may have proved very successful in increasing the contribution of researchers to L2 classrooms as well.

3
Task Selection

Introduction

One key issue in TBLT is task selection for both teaching and assessment purposes. However, opinions differ among TBLT proponents with respect to the procedures by which tasks are selected. As was highlighted in Chapter 1, we now perceive a task as "both an input and an interactional construct" (Mackey, 1999, p. 583). According to Nunan (1991), "task selection should occur with reference both to target task rationale and psycholinguistic principles" (p. 282). Nunan's approach obviously presents a means for defining input in terms of target tasks and for specifying the type of social interaction which would trigger acquisitional processes. Nevertheless, Widdowson's (1990) arguments about synthetic syllabuses and communication probably holds true about tasks as well:

> But a notional/functional syllabus is of itself no more communicative than a "structural" one. Communication is what may or may not be achieved through classroom activity... So I do not see that there is anything paradoxical or perverse in saying there is no such thing as a communicative syllabus. (p. 130)

In TBLT, the mono-episodic interactive oral communication task is pivotal. Language-based synthetic syllabuses (Wilkins, 1976), whether based on criteria such as possible needs or possible difficulty, are substituted by target tasks, also based on needs, which are altered into task types, and then into pedagogic tasks (Long & Crookes, 1992, 1993; Nunan, 1991). The procedures of task selection are seemingly based on "a principled approach to content selection"

(Long & Crookes, 1992, p. 45) and sequenced with respect to difficulty or gradual approximations to the target. Whereas task difficulty and sequencing are the subject of the next chapter, the ways content can be included in a task-based course are the focus of the present chapter. This chapter will underline how teachers can select tasks that cater to the target needs of learners taking into account the pedagogic issues, previous experience and learner interests as independent driving forces for task design.

Prabhu's approach: Task selection based on topic

Perhaps one of the most remarkable implementations of a TBLT approach has been Prabhu's (1987) Communicative Language Teaching Project (CLTP) which is also known as the Bangalore Project. Besides indicating the suitability of a task-based syllabus for young and beginning L2 learners, the Bangalore Project was groundbreaking in three crucial ways. Firstly, the tasks did not have the purpose of teaching and learning of language; rather, they emphasized the learners' use and development of their own cognitive skills through the use of the target language to solve problems. Secondly, Prabhu's procedural syllabus of tasks was centered on what was to be carried out in the classroom and not on selected language input for learning. Thirdly, there was no pre-planning of the tasks in the syllabus; they were selected during the teaching and learning by a process of trial and error. In other words, the syllabus in this project was based on topics that were based upon the interests and endeavors of particular learners in particular teaching contexts. To fulfill this objective, content was selected based on the idea that learners needed to make use of their background knowledge and experiences. Studies have also attested the rationale for selecting tasks based on learners' perceived interests or future needs (Lambert, 2017; Lambert *et al.*, 2017). The study by Lambert, Gong and Zhang (2021), for example, explored ways of altering the intentional vocabulary learning activities at an Australian university to enhance learner engagement in the learning process and advance retention. Participants performed two versions of a picture description task that the teachers consistently used to present and practice target vocabulary in their classes. The teacher-generated content version of the task was based on a picture that the Chinese teachers selected which demonstrated the target words, while the learner-generated content versions were based on pictures that each learner selected as being personally meaningful to them and that showed the target words. The results of this study reported that learners had significantly higher recall for words in the learner-generated content version than in the teacher-generated version on both the immediate and the delayed post-tests. Moreover, although memory for lexis tailed off significantly in both conditions, the rate of deterioration was significantly higher for the teacher-generated condition than the learner-generated one.

The pedagogic tasks that are used in CLTP are defined by Prabhu as pieces of logical thinking. Based on this definition, effective tasks need to fulfill five conditions: (1) they should have content that engenders interest and investment in learners, (2) they should be based on learners' background knowledge and experience, (3) they should strive a balance between predictability and unpredictability, (4) they should have a clear outcome, and (5) they should have a clear criterion for success. Pedagogic tasks that satisfy all these criteria were chosen in the Bangalore Project to reinforce each topic area identified for the syllabus (e.g., working out the money needed to purchase a number of things such as school stationery, vegetables from given price lists and needs—see Prabhu (1987, pp. 140-45) for further examples). One point worthy of highlighting here is that the tasks advocated by Prabhu also align with the criteria of 'tasks' set by Ellis (see Chapter 1) since they were meaning-based, were based on a gap that demanded linguistic processing, required learners to make use of their own linguistic resources in performing them and led to a communicative outcome beyond producing language for its own sake.

Long's approach: Task selection based on needs analysis

In Long's (1985, 2015) approach to TBLT syllabus design, tasks constitute the core of the syllabus based on which it should be conceptualized, arranged, and assessed. This view is clearly opposed to that by Prabhu which considered the use of tasks as means to the development of a general linguistic competence. In fact, what Long emphasizes in his approach to task selection is the ability of learners to enact particular tasks. Ellis *et al.* (2020) regard Long's approach advantageous since it benefits the syllabus designer in different ways. They argue that syllabuses that target the development of language capacities have to acknowledge the universal, natural, and changeable processes involved in language development which are difficult to assess in terms of established stages for all learners. However, as Ellis *et al.* stress, syllabuses that address the ability to enact particular real-world tasks are likely to get around this challenge through "subordinating language to what it is used to accomplish, namely tasks" (p. 185).

As the basis of the syllabus, tasks in Long's approach are selected through needs analysis (Long, 2015). It is only on the basis of the findings of a good needs analysis that, according to Long (2005), a TBLT syllabus can be designed around characteristic pedagogical tasks sequenced in ideal ways. The conduction of a needs analysis in TBLT also leads to gaining information about: (1) the task (what the learner needs to be able to do in the L2), and (2) the language (the language needed to carry out the task without the language that has already been acquired by the learner) (Brown, 2009; Long, 2005). Irrespective of its fundamental role in TBLT curricula, existing instances of needs analysis for TBLT programs are not copious which might be attributed to several issues as noted by Gonzalez-Lloret (2015); (a) needs analysis is wrongly presumed to consist of questions solely for learners about their future language use, along with the doubt that learners are not able to provide helpful answers, (b) teachers responsible for language curriculum rely on ready-made textbooks to have the essential materials without being concerned about the specificities of their program or learners; or (c) there might be difficulties, lack of support, and time commitment that are needed for an effective needs analysis to be effectively performed.

In discussing how tasks can be used as a unit of analysis in L2 course design, Long (2000) differentiates between three levels of task analysis. The first is the analysis of target tasks or the things that individuals perform in everyday life such as making or canceling a hotel or plane reservation. Such target tasks, based on Long, are the result of task-based needs analyses. Following this, the target tasks should be categorized into task types or more abstract, superordinate classes such as making or canceling a reservation in order to present a foundation for designing courses to satisfy the needs of diverse groups of learners without the need to involve each target task individually. The last stage refers to the development of pedagogic tasks or the materials and activities learners actually perform in the classroom, probably filling out or changing a reservation form while listening to a sample telephone call or role-playing customers and clerks who are making or canceling reservations. The goal of designing and grading pedagogic tasks is to encompass each task type and provide opportunities for learners to come up with the distinct dimensions of their L2 ability crucial to perform the tasks that they will encounter in their lives and careers.

The study by Lambert (2010) provides examples of how the task selection principles can be put to practice in understanding the needs of English majors in Japan. Lambert's needs analysis relied on five sources of information: job placement records, interviews with two experienced informants, an open-item survey of alumni with an email survey of a subgroup of these, and a closed-item mail survey of graduates. From the data, five tasks were recognized as highly important for respondents both in business and education fields: locating information, translating documents, summarizing information, editing documents, and interpreting between speakers). Following this preliminary categorization, a large number of yet more abstract task types in accordance with Long's suggestion (e.g., finding information, translating from English to Japanese, editing English documents, etc.) were developed. Lambert's study and its findings strongly suggest that it is realistic to develop a single task-based program to meet the English-related business and educational needs of college learners. In addition to this study, there exist a number of useful guidelines to follow for embarking on a needs analysis (e.g., Altschuld & Witkin, 2000; Brown, 2009; Graves, 2000; Jonassen *et al.*, 1999; Long, 2005; Mackey, 1978; Richterich, 1983; Tarone & Yule, 1989; Witkin & Altschuld, 1995) introducing a variety of methods (surveys, questionnaires, interviews, observations, etc.) to analyze the language needs and select the language tasks.

Robinson's approach: Task selection based on cognitive, ability and affective needs

Robinson (2011) both follows and departs from Long's (1985, 2015) approach to task selection. The convergence of opinions occurs in the definition of task as what L2 learners do in the real world in order to establish what kind of tasks learners would need to perform in the classroom. This position, therefore, necessitates the conduction of needs analysis in the way that Long promotes. Nevertheless, what distinguishes Robinson's (2011) approach to task selection from Long's approach is the analysis of other task conditions such as the cognitive, ability and affective issues which, according to Robinson, affect task performance. Hence, in Robinson's approach, the selection of tasks adheres to the analyses of task dimensions in three stages. The first stage refers to the conduction of a preliminary "behavioral analysis" of tasks in order to determine the target tasks and their communicative features. According to Robinson, behavioral analysis leads to several important pieces of information about target tasks including: (a) a collection target tasks, (b) the communicative conditions of target tasks and learners' roles in performing them, (c) possible subtasks the target tasks come with, (d) task performance procedure, (e) target-like models of completed tasks, and (f) measures of task performance. Based on this information, the syllabus is developed including the contextual and communicative demands that determine the way language is used in the classroom. Ellis *et al.*'s (2020) behavioral analysis aids the identification of the goal orientation of tasks (open/closed, convergent/divergent), the distribution of task-essential information between learners (one-way/two-way), the number of partners in task performance, their role (productive/receptive), and the outcome of the task (meaning negotiation or a lack thereof).

The second stage pertains to an information theoretic analysis of the "cognitive demands" that tasks impose on learners so as to arrive at an effective sequencing of tasks into syllabuses and thus enhance L2 learning. In this stage, the way information in input, output and interaction is processed lays the groundwork for the classification of tasks in the syllabus. As Ellis *et al.* (2020) also noted, not enough is known about the way this analysis needs to be done. Yet, Robinson draws on Skehan's (1998) hypothesis with respect to the selection of tasks based on the cognitive demands of tasks. This issue is closely related to Robinson's approach to sequencing tasks based on whether they direct or disperse learners' cognitive capacities during task performance, which is the focus of Chapter 4 in this book. To explicate how attention is allotted to different areas of performance during language production, Skehan (1998) presents an exemplar-based and a rule-based system. The exemplar-based system includes discrete lexical items and ready-made formulaic chunks that can easily and quickly be retrieved and lead to fluent language use. In contrast, the rule-based system consists of abstract illustrations of the basic patterns of language. These patterns demand more processing and therefore are used in more controlled but less fluent language, which Tarone (1983) calls "the careful style of language". Skehan argues that learners draw on the exemplar-based system when producing fluent language but the rule-based system when producing accurate and complex language. Complexity and accuracy are distinct since accurate language is produced when learners attempt to use the existing resources in a controlled way to prevent errors, whereas complex language is produced when learners take risks to restructure. According to this view, there is a possibility that trade-offs occur between fluency, accuracy, and complexity (between accuracy and complexity in particular) and thus, attending to one of these areas would be at the expense of the other (Ellis, 2005). For teaching purposes, Skehan stresses that tasks which push learners towards switching between both types of processing need to be well-adjusted in the syllabus to facilitate learners' dual-mode processing abilities. Thus, the production of fluent language would not be traded-off at the expense of complexity and accuracy. Accordingly, Robinson (2011) claims that an information-theoretic analysis is helpful in selecting tasks that have suitable cognitive demands for all learners through the manipulation of features in the design of tasks (see Chapter 4 for a more detailed discussion).

In the third stage of task selection, an "ability analysis" is done to clarify how the distinct aptitudes and motivational characteristics of learners would mediate their task performance (Robinson, 2011). Robinson (2011) underlines the crucial role of individual difference variables in task performance contending that tasks can be designed in ways that would be a better fit to some learners than others. This last stage in task selection, thus, entails the analysis of both the ability (aptitude) and affective (motivation) dimensions of tasks to become appropriate to the individual differences of learners (Ellis *et al.*, 2020). Robinson pinpoints aptitude types that can influence task performance and learning: (1) working memory resources (e.g., tasks that do not provide visual support during performance are likely to suit learners with higher working memory capacity); (2) executive control (tasks that necessitate dual-tasking are more appropriate for learners who can alternate quickly from one task to another); (3) causal reasoning ability (tasks that demand the organization of complex opinions fit learners with high causal reasoning ability); (4) sensitivity to the mental states of others (tasks that want learners to contemplate about the different behaviors of individuals require a high level of sensitivity to the mental states of others). In addition, Robinson mentions a number of other factors such as output anxiety, self-efficacy, self-regulation, openness to experience or tolerance of ambiguity as potential influencers of learners' task performance. For instance, Robinson's (2007) study demonstrated that when learners engaged in oral production tasks in pairs, their output anxiety correlated consistently negatively with the use of complex speech structures. Nevertheless, despite Robinson's arguments about the importance of optimizing and uniting learning achievement on tasks through corresponding learners of distinct characteristics with tasks suitable to their affect and ability, thereby decreasing individual difference variations in aptitude and affect, there is no clarification on how such tasks could be integrated into task-based syllabuses (Ellis *et al.*, 2020). Therefore, there are certain challenges to the feasibility of Robinson's approach to task selection since as Ellis *et al.* (2020, p. 195) explain:

> It is not clear how tasks might be matched to learner profiles in practice. Even if researchers were able to demonstrate a finite number of learner types, it would be unrealistic in most language programs to develop and implement separate syllabuses for each of them in order to control for the effects of individual differences on performance and predict the specific learning processes that learners will engage in while performing tasks.

Ellis's approach: Task selection based on learner goals and interests

As noted above, Ellis *et al.* (2020) questioned the practicality of developing a syllabus that can predict all the variability that happens from different groups of learners in different classrooms. In general, Ellis (2018) advocates Prabhus's task-based syllabus design which specifies the factors that impact task complexity such as the linguistic level of the input and open/close task outcome. Ellis suggests the use of a needs analysis in specific purpose courses in order to find out the target tasks that the learners need to be able to carry out as is the case in Long's proposal. However, in general-purpose courses, tasks are recommended to be selected according to the criteria supported by Prabhu, namely learners' familiarity with the tasks and their interest in them. There are, nonetheless, still concerns about the types of topics the tasks should have. Ellis (2018) makes the point that although tasks obviously need to encourage learners' engagement (Philp & Duchesne, 2016), selecting tasks in terms of the topic solely by syllabus designers might not be sufficient and effective since learners need to have their say in the topics that interest them. The choice of topics becomes even more authentic and engaging in content and language integrated learning (CLIL) classrooms where the task-based courses are based on academic subject content and the topics are extracted from the subject syllabi.

One other point worthy of mentioning refers to the role of task in Ellis's proposal for syllabus design. Here, task is seen as a workplan for teachers who can develop it in ways to help their learners cultivate their linguistic profile significantly rather than as a process whereby teachers train learners to carry out a particular number of tasks. In contrast to Prabhu's attention to the development of grammatical competence, Ellis argues that the goal of TBLT is beyond the development of grammar and encompasses the interactive and pragmatic capabilities that would enable learners' effective communication in tasks outside the classroom. In order to put this goal into practice in the classroom, Ellis (2018) suggests that teachers adjust the task as it is performed by the learners to accommodate not only the individual difference variables but also the variations in classroom dynamics to enhance L2 learning.

One last issue that needs to be discussed here is the role of explicit instruction in Ellis' proposal. Unlike the other proposals addressed in this chapter, Ellis acknowledges the role that a more traditional, structural module can play alongside a task-based module in a complete course to ensure a better L2 learning. Ellis proposes a modular curriculum which embraces the task-based component as a principal component, yet also considers a role for a language-related component including a checklist of language forms posing challenges to learners and that can direct explicit language teaching in a way that supplements the task-based part. He puts forward three options for the timing of the structural component in a modular syllabus which are presented in detail in Chapter 5. Briefly, the argument is that these two components—opposed to Long's (2015) claim—are not mismatched. Even if the use of a modular approach may not lead to implicit knowledge, it has a potential to bring about automatized explicit knowledge that can be subsequently turned into implicit knowledge. In sum, then, provided that tasks meet the criteria of taskness as presented in Chapter 1, Ellis considers any approaches to task selection proper based on the goals and interests of the learners in the course for which the syllabus is designed (Ellis *et al.*, 2020).

Kelly and Kelly's (1991, 1996) task-based syllabus is an example of a syllabus that selects tasks according to the materials developer's experience and instinct about the motivating nature of some tasks and their potential to trigger interaction among Japanese English as a foreign language (EFL) learners. This syllabus represents the co-existence of both the task-based and task-supported structural syllabuses in involving learners of diverse motivations and aptitudes in effective oral language use. The criterion for the selection of tasks was not the conduction of an analysis of the contexts that learners would encounter in the future, yet it was chosen according to the experience of the materials developer with regard to the content that could be engaging to the particular group of learners and the opportunities for the development of interactive skills necessary for the future tasks in the real world as well. Furthermore, since one task was not considered to be more significant to the learners than another in this program, the tasks were organized in terms of convenience or intuition.

Conclusion

Advocates of each of these syllabus types in TBLT differ in the justification for their proposals, in the ways they define task, in whether they opt for a formal needs analysis to identify syllabus content, in ways tasks are selected, and in the methodological options, such as explicit instruction and a group work. Their approaches may well vary in other areas as well, but complete and comparable declarations are not available for these proposals on several issues such as testing. This might partly be due to the lack of rigorous field evaluations to put these proposals into sufficient practice. To conclude this chapter, it will be helpful to overview the strengths and weaknesses of each approach to task selection.

The approach presented by Long (1985, 2015) stresses the essence of learners' ability to carry out tasks that are likely to be faced by learners in the real-world. Accordingly, the target tasks that learners need to complete determine both the tasks to be included in the syllabus as well as their organization. Learners' endeavors to carry out the tasks successfully result in their learning the language vital to perform tasks. Targeting task learning instead of language in this way precludes variability in language learning and offers a criterion-based learning outcome for learners mirroring what they aim at achieving outside of the classroom (Ellis *et al.*, 2020).

Nevertheless, it should be noted that the development of competence to solely perform particular tasks is not what the learners and policy makers strive for. The objective of language learning is mostly the development of general abilities that advanced level speakers make use of to enact tasks. To solve this problem, Robinson's (2011) approach to task-based syllabus design intends to identify the cognitive and affective requirements of tasks. Robinson attempts to envisage the language learning processes that happen during the performance of tasks. However, in real classroom settings particularly those with obligated curriculum and tests, it is not feasible for L2 practitioners to predict language learning processes for all learners.

Lastly, Ellis (2018, p. 274) supports "a modular syllabus that gives primacy to pure TBLT throughout but allows for the inclusion of explicit instruction once basic competence has been established as a means of helping learners overcome persistent learning problems."

Ellis has taken a similar approach as Prabhu (1987) has done in highlighting the role of teachers in specifying the details of L2 development on tasks based on their knowledge of their specific groups of learners. Ellis argues that "the syllabus should not function to dictate the procedures used in the classroom, but that it should provide teachers with resources and freedom to address the needs of learners differing in motivation and aptitudes as well as fluctuations in classroom dynamics" (Ellis *et al.*, 2020, p. 207).

4
Task Complexity and Task Sequencing

Introduction

Task complexity and task sequencing are at the heart of TBLT research and pedagogy: research empirically tests theoretical claims that sequencing tasks based on increasing complexity can promote L2 learning opportunities (e.g., Baralt et al., 2014; Robinson & Gilabert, 2007; Skehan & Foster, 2001), and pedagogical frameworks identify ways of putting these research-supported principles into practice in the classroom (e.g., Ellis, 2003; Skehan, 1998; Willis, 1996). The concept of task complexity was introduced in order to set up criteria for sequencing tasks in a syllabus from easy/simple to difficult/complex in a reasoned way that would enhance L2 development (Baralt et al., 2014). Hence, adopting some criteria to grade and sequence pedagogic tasks is vital for the facilitation of both language performance, namely access to and successful deployment of existing L2 knowledge under increasingly demanding processing conditions, as well as language development concerning the necessity of learners not just using their knowledge of L2 more effectively to be successful on target tasks, but also learning new L2 knowledge (Robinson, 2007). Nevertheless, sequencing has posed challenges for both synthetic and analytic syllabi. As noted by Long (2007), for synthetic, grammar-oriented syllabi, materials are normally organized based on the designer's intuition and experience about morphosyntactic and phonological linguistic complexity or by lexical frequency for corpus-based materials. On the other hand, task-based approaches commonly integrate both a content rationale, for instance, arrangements based on thematic relationships, and a complexity rationale, where tasks are arranged from least to most complex (Norris, 2009). In other words, sequencing decisions for TBLT are made using first-hand knowledge about particular groups of learners coupled with an understanding of the communication needs and learning opportunities entailed within different language use tasks (Norris, 2009). The steps in the learning process represented by pedagogic tasks can be arranged from simpler to more complex by exploring the complexity of a task and the task difficulty for individual learners (Long, 2007). However, defining complexity and difficulty is a complicated and challenging task in and of itself. In this chapter, I will discuss the light theories of task complexity and the resulting studies shed on the issue of task sequencing in the language classroom.

Prabhu's approach

One of the proposals for task sequencing in a TBLT syllabus is that of Prabhu's (1987) Bangalore Communicative Teaching Project in India. Prabhu suggested tasks be sequenced based on several criteria which he referred to as "rough measures of cognitive complexity" (p. 47) (see Figure 4.1). The first criterion concerns the amount of information that needs to be handled and proposes that the larger the amount of information (e.g., a few rules in contrast to numerous rules in rule-based tasks), the more difficult the task is. Secondly, Prabhu considers the "amount" of reasoning needed in a task as a factor affecting the task difficulty such that the more the number of steps entailed in the deduction, inference, or calculation towards the outcome, the more challenging the task is predicted to be. The third criterion is related to the degree of accuracy which means that the greater precision for the terms needed to communicate an idea, the more difficult the task becomes. The fourth criterion underlines the degree of learners' familiarity with the goals and limitations of the kind included in the task. The more the learners have knowledge of the words for the completion of a task, the easier the task is. Lastly, Prabhu (1987, pp. 87–88) noted that "working with concepts is more difficult than working with the names of objects or actions," thereby recommending the degree of abstractness as a criterion that can make tasks easy or difficult. In sum, then, Prabhu argues that tasks in a procedural syllabus need to be intellectually challenging enough to uphold learners' interest, for that is what keeps learners' endeavors at task completion, directs them towards a focus on meaning and, as part of that process, involves them in dealing with the linguistic demands of the task (Prabhu, 1987). Opinion-gap followed by information-gap and particularly reasoning-gap tasks were preferred in the Bangalore project. In this approach, it is vital that learners identify a task difficult but also feasible or what Prabhu (1987) terms a "reasonable challenge" (p. 55).

Degree of difficulty

− ⟶ +

Few elements	AMOUNT OF INFORMATION	Many elements
Few steps	AMOUNT OF REASONING	Many steps
Precise terms not needed	DEGREE OF PRECISION	Precise terms needed
Unfamiliar	DEGREE OF FAMILIARITY	Familiar
Objects and actions	DEGREE OF ABSTRACTNESS	Concepts

Figure 4.1 *Prabhu's task complexity criteria (1987, p. 47)*

Methodologically speaking, teacher's practice of putting a "reasonable challenge" into a sequence, whether in a lesson plan or a unit, is decided by the teacher's "commonsense judgment":

> ...tasks within a given sequence...were ordered by a commonsense judgment of increasing complexity, the later tasks being either inclusive of the earlier ones or involving a larger amount of information, or an extension of the kind of reasoning done earlier. (Prabhu, 1987, p. 39)

Therefore, the reasonable challenge is based on (1) the teachers' evaluations of learners' task performance and competencies which are generally identified in the task feedback stage, based on homework grading after class, and on (2) the learners' attitudes towards the task which can be specified during class time, necessitating teacher's online-decision-making about what to include or exclude in a task (Baralt *et al.*, 2014). The criterion used by teachers to evaluate a task's reasonable challenge is based on performance such that half of the learners should succeed on half of the task, demonstrated by their markings on their work (Prabhu, 1987). Prabhu considered this as a sufficient way of evaluating learners' development, which also directed the design of sequences, that is how many tasks of the same type need to be increased in complexity until learners start to get bored.

A major drawback of Prabhu's proposal for task complexity lies in depending on teachers' real-time judgments, along with their approval of how "approximately half the learners in the class" seem to be performing on "approximately half the task" during class time (Prabhu, 1987, p. 56). Thus, this procedure for measuring task complexity to inform task sequencing is limited due to its ambiguity of what 'approximately half the class' means and also because of not constituting a methodologically practical way for teachers to employ in a consistent way in the classroom. Moreover, Prabhu's description of a task's "reasonable challenge" does not clarify what makes one task easier than another, leaving the basis on which teachers make decisions of presenting learners with more complex tasks unclear (Baralt *et al.*, 2014).

Long's approach

Long and Crookes (1992) and later on Long (2015, 2016) have suggested using a predetermined syllabus with tasks as units for sequencing the syllabus. As noted in Chapter 1, Long stresses the essence of conducting a need analysis to determine target tasks that learners will need to do in real-life contexts, developing task types from target tasks, and finally designing and sequencing pedagogic tasks according to the complexity of the tasks to develop a coherent task-based syllabus. In addressing the sequencing criteria, Long and Crookes wrote that pedagogic tasks should be sequenced by "complexity," so that they increasingly "approximate" the target tasks that merited their inclusion in the syllabus in the first place. Long and Crookes (1992) did not suggest an explicit taxonomy for sequencing tasks; nevertheless, their conceptualization of task complexity and the factors causing task complexity can be inferred from their suggestions:

> The number of steps involved, the number of solutions to a problem, the number of parties involved and the saliency of their distinguishing features, the location (or not) of a task in displaced time and space, the amount and kind of language required, the number of sources competing for attention, and other aspects of the intellectual challenge a pedagogic task poses... (p. 44).

Long and Crookes also underscored the important role of pedagogic options that are used to implement tasks (e.g., open versus closed, planned versus unplanned, whole-class versus small-group interactions) to modulate task complexity. In a similar vein, Gilabert (2005) highlighted the necessity of collecting information via needs analysis about different options such as the number of elements in each task, the reasoning demands in each task, the number of steps in task performance, the degree of displaced, past time reference, and the time given for preparation to sequence tasks in a task-based syllabus according to increasing complexity. To clarify, in Long's approach to task sequencing, a simple task can be a task in which language is not necessarily required such as in painting a fence. To perform the task, brush, paint, sandpaper, and a fence are needed. The steps are collecting materials, sanding the wood, painting the wood, and leaving it to dry. The purpose is to make the fence look better, and the task has a concrete and perceptible outcome. Language would not necessarily be required for this task. In contrast, Gilabert (2005) presents an example of a complex task in which language is required: interviewing a source in the field of journalism. This task encompasses several steps or sub-tasks such as obtaining information with regard to the source, getting in touch with the source, detailing the interview, arranging the interview, interviewing the source, and writing the transcript or an article according to the interview.

In sum, Long's approach to task sequencing is prominent in terms of how to identify which tasks to present learners in a task-based syllabus beginning with a needs analysis, and he supports the sequencing of pedagogic tasks in increasingly complex forms so that they approach real-world target tasks. The limitation of this approach, however, is that there are no specific suggestions about how to implement sequencing in line with the complexity level of a task.

Ellis's approach

Ellis (1987, 2003) has suggested that two parallel types of tasks—unfocused and focused—be used in task-based and task-supported language teaching. Whereas an unfocused task makes meaning primary with learners being able to use their own linguistic resources to complete the task, a focused task can be employed to stretch learners' linguistic resources with meaning still being the focus of the task, yet form (e.g., grammar, vocabulary, and/or pragmatics) is discussed by learners in task performance. In task-supported language teaching, the curriculum is sequenced according to linguistic items and tasks are used to present situational practice of the linguistic/notional/functional items that are provided and practiced before their production in the last stage of instruction. In contrast, in task-based language teaching, tasks form the units of the syllabus and language learning stems incidentally from task performance and from pre-task, during-task, and post-task exploitations (Skehan, 2014, 2016). Unlike Ellis's (2003) recommendation that both task-supported and task-based language teaching need to be used in language teaching, Long (2015, 2016), Robinson (2011), and Skehan (2014) are against task-supported language teaching. It is in TBLT that developing criteria for task difficulty and sequencing is an unresolved issue (Long, 2015, 2016).

Ellis (2003) has put forward four criteria (i.e., input, conditions, processes, and outcomes) for task difficulty (see Table 4.1). Input is the information that is required for task completion; conditions refer to the type of task performance (e.g., monologic vs. dialogic); processes pertain to cognitive processes entailed (e.g., inferencing); and outcome refers to whether the task output is simple or complex. These four criteria can be manipulated by task designers to develop tasks of differing degrees of difficulty. Similar to Long (2015, 2016), Long and Crookes (1992), Robinson (2011) and Skehan (1998, 2014, 2016), Ellis (2003, 2013) has also underlined the essence of employing methodological options (e.g., pre-task planning time or pre-teaching vocabulary in the pre-task stage), which are used to implement task-based pedagogy, in modulating the complexity/difficulty of tasks in accordance with the learners' proficiency level. In spite of some divergences in their proposals, these scholars have proposed the design of tasks based on task difficulty/complexity criteria and their grading from easy to difficult to develop a task-based syllabus, and that methodological options are advocated as ways of further modulating the task complexity/difficulty and implementing the task-based syllabus.

Ellis's task-based syllabus, similar to that by Prabhu (1987), also encourages teachers to promote L2 learning through supporting learners with different levels of motivation and aptitude based on their experience with their learners as well as the learners' behaviors as they perform the tasks in the classroom (Ellis et al., 2020). In sum, although Ellis's approach does not offer a guide for how to sequence tasks, his grading concept basically seems to be an attempt to verify cognitive complexity growth in individual tasks.

Table 4.1 *Ellis's criteria for sequencing tasks (Ellis, 2003, pp. 217–228)*

Criterion	Easy	Difficult
Input ⟶ Nature of the input provided in the task 1. Medium	pictorial ⟶ written	⟶ oral
2. Code complexity	high frequency vocabulary; short and simple sentences	low frequency vocabulary; complex sentence structure

3. Cognitive complexity
  a. information type
  b. amount of information
  c. degree of structure
  d. context dependency
	static ⟶ dynamic
	few elements/ relationships
	well-defined structure
	here-and-now
		⟶ abstract
		many elements/ relationships
		little structure
		there-and-then

4. Familiarity of information	familiar	unfamiliar
Conditions ⟶ way in which the information is presented to learners and the way in which it is to be used 1. Interactant relationship (negotiation of meaning)	two-way	one-way
2. Task demands	single task	dual task
3. Discourse mode in which learners must perform the task	dialogic	monologic

Processes ⟶ the nature of the cognitive operations and discourse that the task requires
1. **Cognitive operations**
    a. **type**
 	
    b. **reasoning need**
	exchanging information
	
	reasoning few steps involved
		⟶ exchanging opinions
		
		many steps involved

Outcomes ⟶ the nature of the product that results from performing the task 1. **Medium** 2. **Scope** 3. **Discourse mode of task outcome**	pictorial closed lists, descriptives, narratives, classifications	⟶ written ⟶ oral open ⟶ instructions, arguments

Skehan's approach

Skehan (1998, 2002, 2003, 2009, 2014) and Skehan and Foster (2001) have supported a balanced interlanguage development and postulated that in TBLT there is too much attention to meaning at the expense of form which can result in developing communicative strategies and using lexicalized language in successful communication without sufficient attention to form that can have negative effects on interlanguage development. Viewing language learning from an information-processing perspective, Skehan (1996) highlighted the efficacy of investigating language learning as a three-pronged goal: complexity, accuracy, and fluency (CAF), and has proposed a framework for attaining a balanced L2 development. Skehan (1998, 2014) and Skehan and Foster's (1999, 2001) trade-off hypothesis (TOH)/limited capacity model (LCM) claims that tasks that are more demanding require more attentional resources, thereby leaving less attention to be devoted to linguistic form. Accordingly, this model proposes grading tasks from least to most complex tasks to provide opportunities for learners to focus on both meaning and form.

Skehan's framework to achieve a balanced L2 development underlines the importance of both task sequencing (syllabus) and task implementation (methodology). Skehan (1996) suggested criteria for determining task difficulty consisting of task complexity (syntactic and lexical difficulty), cognitive complexity (content required for successful task performance), cognitive processing (amount of online mental processing required during the task performance), cognitive familiarity (whether the task refers to ready-made solutions), time pressure (the time required for the performance of the task), modality (speaking versus writing), scale (number of participants), stakes (the importance of task performance) and control (participants' potential influence on the way a task is enacted and whether the participants can negotiate the task goals). To elaborate, higher code complexity, cognitive complexity, cognitive processing, communicative stress, scale, and stakes, and lower cognitive familiarity and control make tasks more difficult. Furthermore, Skehan asserts that speaking and listening tasks bring about more pressure and are thus more difficult compared to writing and reading tasks. He suggests that tasks be sequenced from simple to more difficult based on his task difficulty criteria to form a task-based syllabus.

Skehan (1996) posits that "this scheme allows tasks to be analyzed, compared, and best of all, sequenced according to some principled basis" (p. 52). Provided that the tasks are selected effectively, there will be (1) a balance between achieving fluency and accuracy, and (2) restructuring opportunities. The task needs to come with an appropriate difficulty level: "Tasks ... should not be so difficult that excessive mental processing is required simply to communicate any sort of meaning. ... Nor should tasks be so easy that learners are bored" (Skehan, 1996, p. 55). In addition to his framework for analyzing and comparing tasks, Skehan, following Willis (1996), highlights the significance of methodology in order to successfully implement TBLT and argues for the three stages of pre-task, during-task, and post-task activities. He has maintained that teachers can further modulate the difficulty of tasks and attract learners' attention to different dimensions of L2 production (i.e., CAF) through making implementation decisions in the pre-task, during-task, and post-task stages. As one moves to detail, in the pre-task planning stage, teachers can focus learners' attention on complexity by providing them with adequate pre-task planning. Actions can also be taken to adapt the code and cognitive complexity and cognitive processing included in task production. During task performance, the communication stress (time, modality, scale, stakes, and control) can be modulated to attract learners' attention to the intended dimensions of task production. And, with respect to the post-task phase, different techniques including the use of post-task activities such as public performance, task repetition, and reminding the learners that a particular activity will follow the main task performance can be used to draw learners' attention to a specific dimension of L2 production (i.e., CAF), which can in turn result in restructuring, consolidating, and fluency.

To date, Skehan's proposal is one of the most detailed and comprises numerous classroom implementation considerations which have been subject to a wealth of empirical studies which will be overviewed in Part III of the present book. Skehan's work on the cognitive viewpoint for language learning in conjunction with the TBLT methodology considerations have influenced the field to a great extent. Although he provides a means to corroborate that a balanced selection of tasks is used in order to advance development in terms of CAF, his model does not seem to suggest a principled set of criteria for grading tasks. In comparison, Robinson's cognition hypothesis makes much clearer and more straightforward predictions about task complexity which has generated a considerable amount of research (see below).

Robinson's approach

Robinson (2001a, 2001b, 2003, 2005, 2010, 2011a, 2011b) has proposed the Triadic Componential Framework (TCF) for task design and classification and SSARC model (SS = simple, stable; A = automatization; R = restructuring; C = maximum complexity) for task sequencing. He differentiates task complexity from task difficulty defining the former as:

> ...the result of the attentional, memory, reasoning, and other information processing demands imposed by the structure of the task on the language learner. These differences in information processing demands, resulting from design characteristics, are relatively fixed and invariant. (Robinson, 2001a, p. 29)

In contrast to Skehan's LCM, Robinson's cognition hypothesis, operationalized in the TCF (see Figure 4.2), recommends a multiple resources viewpoint on language processing that expects that conceptual demands of the tasks encourage learners to draw on multiple resource pools and process different dimensions of language at the same time. As such, Robinson states that the conceptual demands of more cognitively complex tasks attract learners' multiple attentional resources to complexity and accuracy and facilitate language learning and development. He argues that increasing cognitive task complexity would intensify the conceptual demands of the task which, in turn, would bring about interlanguage development, the use of developmentally more advanced forms of language, and will also lead to accurate L2 production. Robinson's TCF and SSARC model present an explicit way of increasing opportunities for L2 learning through a systematic increase in cognitive demands on learners (Robinson, 2001a, 2005). The framework operationalizes task complexity as cognitive complexity, consisting of both resource-dispersing and resource-directing dimensions, which are concerned with the ways learners' attentional capacities are focused as a function of task design. The resource-directing dimension imposes different degrees of cognitive demands on the attentional resources of the learners. The degree depends on the tasks' conceptual demands such as their reference to past or present events, here and now, few or many elements, and more or fewer reasoning demands. The resource-dispersing dimension imposes procedural demands on the learners' cognitive resources and comprises planning time, prior knowledge of the task, and the number of tasks to be completed, among others. Increasing cognitive complexity together with the resource-dispersing dimension, such as having planning time (+ planning time) to not having planning time (− planning time), is presumed to direct the focus on meaning and automatization of language use and thereby lead to fluency. On the other hand, increasing complexity on the resource-directing dimension draws learners' attention to linguistic form and pushes them towards producing more accurate and complex language to meet the rise in cognitive demands. For instance, by manipulating the resource-directing factor +/− here-and-now, including the present tense in a simple task in the present tense (+ here-and-now) and altering it to the past tense in a more complex version (− here-and-now) would focus learners'

Task Complexity and Task Sequencing

attention to particular linguistic features, thereby theoretically enhancing form-function mapping, accuracy and complexity.

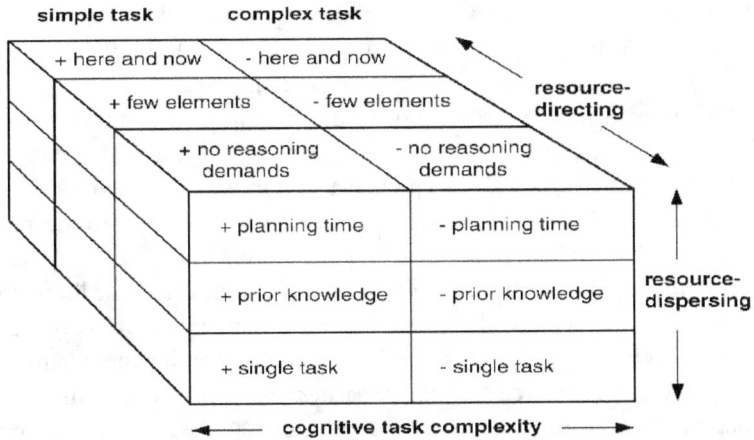

Figure 4.2 *Resource-directing versus resource-dispersing dimensions of cognitive task complexity (Robinson, 2003)*

Whereas the resource-dispersing and resource-directing dimensions are presented in the TCF, the SSARC model offers a step-by-step formula for ways to carry out increasing cognitive complexity and drawing learners' attention along resource-dispersing and directing dimensions. As seen in the following, the model includes three steps with 'i' alluding to the learners' existing interlanguage condition, 'e' to learners' mental effort and 'n' to the encouraged iteration of each step as many times as considered necessary for the specific learners.

Step 1. SS = i × e ('s'rdisp) + ('s'rdir)n
Step 2. A = i × e ('c'rdisp) + ('s'rdir)n
Step 3. RC = i × e ('c'rdisp) + ('c'rdir)n

In the first step, the model proposes the enactment of a task that is both simple ('s') along the resource-dispersing ('rdisp') dimension and simple along the resource directing ('rdir') dimension (e.g., providing planning time [+ planning time] to the learners and in the present tense [+ here-and-now]). The second step necessitates a rise solely in the cognitive complexity of the resource-dispersing dimensions (e.g., eliminating planning time [− planning time] and keeping the present tense [+ here-and-now]). Lastly, in the third step, cognitive complexity is increased along the resource-directing dimension (carrying on with [− planning time] and also moving to [− here-and now], e.g., in the past or future tense). And, each stage may be repeated as needed (Robinson, 2010).

Sequencing tasks from less to more complex is theorized to facilitate instructed SLA for several reasons (Ellis, 2003). Enabling learners to ease into a task sequence and familiarizing them with the content and format is posited to facilitate their attention to meaning and the communicative purpose(s) of the task, while following tasks with greater complexity facilitates learners' attention to the linguistic form within the already created meaningful context (Robinson, 2011a). With respect to learners' interlanguage development, simpler tasks are hypothesized to allow learners to produce pragmatically focused speech and, with more repetition, achieve more syntactic language production, representing language learning in informal contexts. Accordingly, task complexity sequencing is presumed to boost greater processing by learners than detached, unrelated tasks, which may restrict the depth of processing.

Robinson's framework has been subject to a large amount of empirical research (e.g., Baralt *et al.*, 2014a; Robinson, 2011a; Robinson & Gilabert, 2007) and has been generally supported in studies conducted so far (see Jackson & Suethanapornkul, 2013 and Johnson, 2017 for recent meta-analyses). The first meta-analysis by Jackson and Suethanapornkul (2013) revealed that increasing resource-directing features of task complexity had only small impacts on the accuracy (d = 0.28) and the fluency (d = −0.16) of oral language produced. A much larger meta-analysis including more studies and more variables has been conducted by Malicka and Sasayama (2017). They found that resource-dispersing variables had stronger and more consistent relationships with performance than did resource-directing variables. Although none of the resource-directing or resource-dispersing dimensions enhanced all performance areas, the resources-directing dimension (i.e., the there-and-then condition) enhanced structural complexity, and resource-dispersing dimensions (planning, repetition) improved oral accuracy and fluency. These results do not agree with Jackson and

Suethanapornkul's (2013) findings. Whereas they reported higher values for accuracy, Malicka and Sasayama (2017) indicated the highest value for complexity. The results of Johnson's (2017) meta-analysis suggest some consistent impacts of cognitive task complexity manipulation with regard to ±reasoning demands and ±here-and-now. The manipulation of ±here-and-now was associated with small to medium positive effects on the syntactic complexity, accuracy, and fluency of written L2 production. Furthermore, increased attention to the reasoning demands of the writing task led to a tradeoff between complexity, accuracy, and fluency. Although Johnson's findings provide no clear support for or refutation of the cognition hypothesis and its application to L2 writing, they suggest that L2 writers may respond to cognitively more complex tasks not only by producing more complex and accurate language, but also by producing language more fluently. Obviously, then, given that only a handful of task complexity features have received more attention than others and the reliance of many studies on relatively few metrics of CAF, there is a need for more research synthesis and meta-analysis to more closely and widely examine L2 learning as a result of task complexity.

The cognition hypothesis has also triggered a very large number of individual studies. These studies commonly manipulated one or more of the resource-directing variables to examine the impacts of cognitive task complexity on accuracy and complexity. Oftentimes, a resource-directing variable is combined with a resource-dispersing variable, yet this could be a challenging design since the two types of dimensions may lead to opposing predictions (Inoue, 2016). Among these studies, some revealed impacts of task complexity on lexical density (e.g., Niwa, 2000), some on accuracy and fluency but not structural complexity (Robinson, 2001a), others on accuracy but not structural and lexical complexity (Gilabert *et al.*, 2011; Kuiken & Vedder, 2008), and yet others finding no effects (e.g., Michel, 2011). In sum, these studies along with numerous other studies lead to a generalization that task complexity is related to accuracy, yet not both accuracy and complexity particularly in oral production (see Ishikawa, 2007 for a writing-based study). This uniform pattern of results is noteworthy given the central claim of the cognition hypothesis regarding the simultaneous development of both accuracy and complexity. With this in mind, research in this area with both written and oral monologic tasks may wish to explore performances on complex tasks in sequences, spaced over longer periods of time in order to achieve more consistent findings (see the study by Kim and Payant, 2017). That is, instead of performing a single complex task, repeating the performance of complex tasks is likely to prompt the use of more complex language such that the suggested effects of task complexity on pushing the complexity of responses to task demands, and stretching interlanguage, are more evident (Baralt *et al.*, 2014).

The SSARC model has also received some criticism. Ellis *et al.* (2020), for example, consider the formulae vague, without sufficient details about terms such as 'e' for mental effort and 'n' for number of practice opportunities. They also assert that although the model illuminates the sequencing of combinations of resource-directing and resource-dispersing dimensions such as time perspective and planning, it does not make clear "how particular combinations like this would fit into a longer sequence as one would expect from a practical syllabus" (p. 86). Lastly, Ellis *et al.* (2020) also criticize the vagueness of the sequence of stabilize–simplify–automatize–restructure–complexify and its conflicts with some theories of learning. "It seems to propose automatization before restructuring-complexifying, rather than the other way around. Perhaps connected with this, it lacks clarity as to what happens after the restructuring-complexification has taken place. One wonders if there is need for consolidation or practice at this point" (p. 86).

Conclusion

Determining what makes a task more complex, and delineating how tasks should be effectively sequenced from less to more complex, is being heavily explored in instructed SLA. When it comes to rigorously and optimally operationalizing what factors increase the complexity of a task, nevertheless, options proliferate within TBLT. As follows from the review in this chapter, while Skehan (1996) defines task complexity as including code complexity (e.g., linguistic and vocabulary), cognitive complexity (e.g., familiarity of the task) and the communicative stress of the task (time pressure, mode, etc.), Ellis (2003) portrays easy and more difficult tasks regarding the type of input provided to learners (e.g., familiarity of information), conditions of task performance (e.g., discourse mode) and the cognitive processes required of a task and its outcome (e.g., closed or open). Although numerous researchers have emphasized task sequencing and complexity, most agree that the issue is far from resolved (e.g., Long, 1985; Robinson, 2001a, 2001b; Skehan, 1998). This might be because there is an interplay of several factors that affect the complexity of a task, for which there is currently no theory. As noted by Ellis *et al.* (2020), the problem is aggravated when we acknowledge that the complexity of a particular task is a function of not just its design but also the way it is implemented. For example, having the opportunity to plan for the performance of a task before its performance or a lack of such opportunity would influence the cognitive load that the task places on the learner. Therefore, the role played by design variables on task complexity cannot be identified independently of implementation conditions (Ellis *et al.*, 2020). To conclude this section, I would like to call for more research particularly those that depart from using predominantly quantitative approaches to those that adopt qualitative methods. And, as pointed out earlier, investigating the complexity of the task-as workplan on its own bears little implications for a practical classroom syllabus and practice and there is a need to take into account the conditions under which a task is performed. This latter issue is dealt with in detail in the next section.

PART III

TASK IMPLEMENTATION

5
Explicit Instruction in TBLT

Introduction

In addition to using focused tasks as a way of attracting learners' attention to particular linguistic forms, a focus on form can also be implemented methodologically. In this chapter, firstly, a discussion over the necessity of including explicit instruction in TBLT is presented which is based on different proposals by the TBLT commentators. This will lead to a detailed presentation of different proposals for the use of form-focused activities that they advocate to be implemented in different stages of a task-based lesson. In almost all the methods, there are three stages to the use of task, namely a pre-stage, a during-task stage, and a post-task stage, as introduced by Prabhu in 1987. Overall, in the pre-task stage, learners perform activities that prepare them for the performance of an upcoming main task. The during-task stage is where learners actually engage in the performance of the communicative task. Eventually, the post-task entails the activities that follow-up on the previous task performance (Ellis, 2003). Table 5.1 (adapted from Ellis, 2014, pp. 105–106) illustrates the TBLT scholars' diverse positions with respect to the place of an explicit focus on form (FonF) in the TBLT framework. All these positions will be covered in this chapter. This chapter will conclude by explaining whether there can be a place for task-supported language teaching (TSLT) both theoretically and based on the research conducted so far.

Table 5.1 *The place of explicit instruction in the TBLT framework*

Willis (1996)	Long (1985, 1991, 2015)	Skehan (1998)	Ellis (2003)
In the pre-task and post-task phases but not in the main task phase	In the main-task phase	Mainly in the pre-task phase	In all phases of a lesson

The debate over the role of explicit instruction in TBLT

The proponents of TBLT agree that an explicit FonF needs to be included only in the post-task stage of a lesson. Nonetheless, the chief point of disagreement lies in whether explicit instruction can be integrated in the pre-task stage. TSLT presents an explicit instruction of a target structure before the performance of a task. TSLT offers a range of linguistic forms which are initially taught explicitly and then practiced in 'real operating conditions' using tasks in line with skill acquisition theory (DeKeyser, 1998). However, in what Long (2015) advocates as "pure" TBLT, there is no room for explicit instruction prior to the performance of a task since this would be a return to "focus-on-forms," which he defines as an approach to teaching that uses a structural syllabus, explicit instruction and controlled practice exercises (Long, 1991). Thus, in both TSLT and TBLT, tasks as workplans that provide opportunities for using language under real-operating conditions are used, yet with a distinct intended mental set (Ellis, 2019a). In TSLT, a task is used with the purpose of providing learners with opportunities to exhibit the accurate use of an explicitly taught target linguistic structure while attempting to accomplish a communicative outcome. In TBLT, on the other hand, a task intends to provide opportunities for using language naturally to attain a communicative outcome. In both approaches, the expectation is that learners would attend to form but in TSLT learners are directed to focus on a predetermined form while in TBLT focus on form arises incidentally when learners enact the task (Ellis, 2019a).

The debate over the role of explicit instruction in a task-based lesson revolves around two key concepts: the need to ascertain that instruction corresponds to the way learners acquire an L2 and the necessity of taking account of the limitations in diverse teaching contexts (Li *et al.*, 2018). The case for TSLT is based on two propositions. Firstly, the implementation of TBLT in some instructional contexts, particularly those where the L2 is instructed as a foreign in contrast to a second language, faces challenges (Carless, 2012; Littlewood, 2014). Following Adams and Newton (2009), Shehadeh (2012) explains about a list of issues that pose challenges to adopting TBLT in foreign language contexts. He refers to institutional factors (e.g., traditional examinations), teacher factors (e.g., teachers' preference for more traditional, teacher-centered pedagogy), and learner factors (e.g., learners' preference for relying on the teacher as an authority figure). Samuda and Bygate (2008) highlighted that there are distinctions between issues that researchers explore and issues that teachers are interested in; that TBLT is perceived as a "top-down initiative" (p. 192) enforced on teachers by researchers (Van den Branden, 2006); and that researchers oftentimes overlook the difficulties and obstacles that teachers encounter in the local teaching context (Swan, 2005). In fact, several research studies have also confirmed the challenges associated with a successful implementation of TBLT. For example, Erlam (2016) revealed that following their attendance in a year-long in-service training, over half of the 43 secondary school language teachers were still unable to design tasks that could satisfy all the principal criteria of a task. Van de Guchte, Rijlaarsdam, Braaksma, and Bimmel (2017) interviewed five experienced task-based language teachers at a Dutch secondary school with respect to what they thought about the necessity of pre-task grammar instruction. The teachers all expressed that they instructed grammar explicitly prior to asking learners to carry out an oral or a written task. They reasoned that the majority of the other Dutch teachers instructed grammar in their classes, and that they wanted their learners to know the same grammar rules as the other learners did.

The second claim for a task-supported approach is grounded in skill acquisition theory (DeKeyser, 1998, 2015), which posits that learners must have declarative knowledge, which can be learned through pre-task grammar instruction, proceduralized in subsequent skill-specific task performance and then automatized through repeated practice. DeKeyser (1998) stressed the essence of communicative drills, which learners perform with the aid of their declarative knowledge, followed by "more open-ended activities" (p. 60)—that is, tasks—to accomplish automatization. However, such instruction may lead to the automation of declarative knowledge rather than true implicit knowledge, which DeKeyser (2003) advocated are functionally equivalent. In a similar vein, Nunan (2004) also supported the provision of grammar instruction before learners engage in "freer practice" (p. 33) or pedagogical tasks in which they have complete freedom in meaning-making drawing on their own linguistic resources. Nevertheless, Nunan pointed out that grammar instruction should happen following learners' exposure to authentic input via listening practice and controlled practice of vocabulary so the learner can "see the relationship between communicative meaning and linguistic form" (p. 32). Quintessentially, Nunan's approach is an alternative version of the presentation–practice–production (PPP) approach, which is based on skill acquisition theory.

As a strong opponent of pre-task grammar instruction, Long (2015) claimed that any approach needs to be "psycholinguistically plausible" (p. 7), and that TBLT was generally in line with SLA research findings over the past 40 years. Long's reasoning for TBLT is fundamentally based on the findings of the morpheme acquisition studies (Krashen, 1981), which indicated the learners' pursuing a scheduled and unchanging path in L2 grammar learning. This predetermined path implies that it is impossible to provide grammar instruction on a preselected linguistic structure as learners may not be prepared to learn the structure in question. He also queried whether the explicit knowledge learned through TSLT could be developed into implicit knowledge through practice on the grounds that learners' "internal syllabus" and the "natural processes" of acquisition are not considered.

Although Ellis (2003) and Willis and Willis (2007) also object to grammar instruction in the pre-task stage for orienting learners to treat a task as a grammar exercise than a communicative task, Skehan (1998) stands between the two polarized approaches—TSLT and TBLT—by supporting a weak form of TBLT where learners' attention is attracted to linguistic forms by means of planning or other form-focusing strategies. Skehan advocates the use of guided planning by providing learners with a handout explaining the usage of a specific linguistic feature. Although guided planning includes explicit information about the linguistic structure, it does not constitute an explicit type of grammar instruction, and therefore can be considered as a weak form of TBLT.

Lastly, Lantolf (2009) also questioned Long's argument for the existence of a natural and fixed route of acquisition signifying the importance of explicit instruction and intentional language learning as not just desirable but essential for L2 development. Lantolf supports the learnability of any grammatical structure at any time on the condition that it is properly mediated. Therefore, Lantolf's argument counters the research that refers to the weakness of instruction in switching the path learners pursue. The study by Zhang and Lantolf (2015) was carried out to test Pienemann's (1985) teachability hypothesis which holds that instruction needs to target a particular linguistic form only if that feature is next in line to be learned with respect to the natural sequence of acquisition. They taught adult learners of Chinese an L2 grammatical feature that was well ahead of their existing developmental stage and found that artificially creating a developmental route different from the one predicted by natural developmental sequences was possible. These findings approve the claims of Vygotsky's developmental education stressing the mediation of learners' conscious understanding of meaning-form mappings (Zhang & Lantolf, 2015). Briefly, Vygotsky's (1978) sociocultural theory emphasizes the mutual interactional behavior of an expert and a learner (or between learners) where the expert assists or scaffolds the novice to perform a skill or a linguistic structure that they cannot perform by themselves. There are several other studies that also attest variable developmental routes (see Ellis, 2015). In a nutshell, although mainstream TBLT—as promoted by Long (2015)—is grounded in cognitive-interactionist theories that give precedence to incidental acquisition and FonF, sociocultural SLA favors explicit instruction given that it follows Vygotskian principles. Indeed, sociocultural theorists endorse TSLT where tasks lead to the application of conscious linguistic knowledge acquired through explicit instruction in meaning-focused activity.

To sum up this section, TSLT and TBLT draw on diverse ways of using tasks in a lesson with the former relying on a synthetic, structural syllabus and an accuracy-oriented methodology and the latter using an analytic, task-based syllabus and a fluency-oriented methodology. In spite of the theoretical and instructional differences, they both share a common assumption about the necessity of a FonF procedure, yet with disputes about its proper place in the lesson. In the following sections, I will elaborate the approaches advocated by different TBLT commentators regarding the best task stage for a FonF, followed by Ellis's (2018, 2019a) proposal for a modular curriculum that combines task-based and structured components.

FonF in the pre-task stage

In Willis's (1996) model, the pre-task stage provides the teacher with the opportunity to outline the task, examine the topic and highlight useful words and phrases. At this stage, then, an introduction to the topic and task is presented in order to activate the relevant schemata. Learners may also listen to others carrying out the same or a similar task, offering them a model which provides useful vocabulary. Other activities that could trigger learners' awareness of linguistic features could comprise "reading and talking about texts and picking out words and phrases" that may be overviewed at the post-task stage (for more examples see Willis 1996, pp. 43–45). Learners may also be given time to prepare for the task at this stage, which positively impacts their language production (see Skehan, 2016 for a succinct review of research findings in this area). It should be noted that even though the introduction of language is not aimed at teaching specific grammatical structures, activating helpful words and phrases can act as opportunities for a "focus on form to be set in motion, and for noticing to occur" (Skehan, 1998, p. 127). Hence, the main goal for this stage is to ensure the processing burden during task performance and monitoring is declined and the learner's attention is freer to be dedicated to any unexpected content and/or form-related problems that may arise, thereby enhancing the chances of successful task completion in both quantitative and qualitative terms (Khezrlou et al., 2017; Sadeghi et al., 2017).

In contrast to Willis, Ellis (2003, 2009a) argues that FonF can figure in all three phases of the TBLT framework. For the pre-task stage, he recommends some of the same activities Willis does, yet warns of the danger of providing models or pre-teaching the target structure of a focused task. After being exposed to the model, Ellis argues, learners may consider the subsequent task as an exercise to practice the target linguistic features they have noticed in the modeled task (Ellis, 2003). As a result, learners might become obsessed with the use of the linguistic target, thereby restricting their linguistic choices and threatening the 'meaning primary' principle of a task. Ellis points out the necessity of teachers being aware of the degree to which learners are "primed to attend to specific aspects of the model" (p. 246). Willis and Willis (2007) expressed a similar concern:

> We should not allow form-focused activities to detract from a focus on meaning. If we have spent time presenting and practicing specific forms immediately before introducing a task, then it is likely that the learners will be concerned to display the target forms rather than concentrate on getting the message across. The task is likely to become a "further practice" of form activity. (p. 113)

The last pre-task FonF option is providing learners with time to plan their task which is promoted by Skehan (1998), Ellis (2003) and Willis (1996) as an effective pre-task activity (see Chapter 6 of the present book for a detailed discussion). Skehan (1996) argues that pre-task planning decreases learners' cognitive load because it releases them from "having to think of too many things at a time when both composing thoughts and producing speech" (p. 25). This freed-up attention may then be dedicated to linguistic form, thereby leading to a more accurate performance (Foster & Skehan, 1996). In addition to enhancements in accuracy, planning time may also develop L2 fluency or complexity (Crookes, 1989; Foster & Skehan, 1996). Planning time may be provided in two different ways, either guided or unguided. In the guided type, learners can select where to pay their attention to (Ortega, 1999), while in the unguided type, their attention is allotted to particular dimensions of the task performance, for example to either form or content (Foster & Skehan, 1999) or to both form and content (Sangarun, 2005). Finally, Skehan also makes similar remarks as Ellis regarding the effectiveness of FonF in the pre-task. Ellis argued that pre-task activities "can help to create conditions that will make tasks work for acquisition', but cannot, 'fine-tune learners' performance of a task..." (p. 249). In the same vein, Skehan (1996) made a case that pre-task work creates conditions that may result in learning but may not immediately lead to learning. Skehan elaborates that we cannot be sure that the language that learners were directed to in the pre-task will occur during subsequent task performance (see Chapter 6).

The concerns expressed by these scholars may mean that the explicit pre-task FonF leads to opportunities for learners to practice instead of using the target structure, making the performance of the task far from natural. Several studies have explored the effectiveness of focused tasks without pre-task instruction in stimulating the use of particular structures. These studies have led to unequivocal conclusions. The studies conducted by Doughty and Varela (1998) and Mackey (1999), for example, reported that the focused tasks caused the use of both more attempted and accurate use of the targeted structures. On the other hand, Samuda (2001) found that learners did not use target structures during the performance of the task and only after the presentation of the verbs in the lesson did they begin trying to use them. Boston's (2010) use of an opinion-gap narrative task as a focused task was not successful in helping learners attempt to use the target structure (passive voice). These unsatisfactory findings underline the challenges involved in relying on the use of a focused task on its own to make the use of the targeted structures 'essential' in contrast to just 'useful' or 'natural' (Loschky & Bley-Vroman, 1993). There is the danger of avoidance when the target structure lies well beyond the learners' developmental stage.

The inclusion of an explicit FonF in the pre-task stage may potentially induce the use of a target feature during the performance of a focused task. However, the direction of attention to the linguistic feature may also adversely influence the general specificities of the language produced. Several studies have intended to address these possibilities through comparing the impacts of enacting the same task with and without pre-task grammar instruction. In De la Fuente's (2006) study, learners were exposed to explicit instruction of Spanish words, were involved in controlled practice, and then carried out a free meaning-based production task which necessitated the use of the target words. Overall, the results indicated that the use of pre-task explicit instruction could not induce the use of the target words in the free production stage of the lesson which was attributed to the nature of task in not making the use of the words essential. Similarly, the use of a dictogloss task after some explanations about the target structure in Kowal and Swain's (1997) study led to a minimal use of the target structure, leading Kowal and Swain to conclude that "the dictogloss approach might be better suited to promoting syntactic processing skills in general than as a means for drawing attention to a particular grammar form" (p. 300). The results of these studies refer to the learners' skills in avoiding the use of items targeted by pre-task instruction if they are not essential for performing the task or if they are too complicated for the learners' existing developmental level.

In contrast, there are other studies that have reported the significant effectiveness of pre-task explicit instruction in enhancing the use of the target structure. The study by Li, Ellis, and Kim (2018) investigated the role of pre-task explicit instruction in Chinese EFL learners' L2 learning. Participants performed two communicative tasks that exposed them to English passive voice—the target structure. It was found that pre-task instruction led to greater gains in explicit knowledge as measured by a grammaticality judgment test, but not on an elicited imitation test that measured implicit knowledge. In another study, Wang and Wang (2014) found that university learners who received grammar instruction before a writing task reported that such instruction benefitted both their writing and editing abilities. Corroborating these findings, Shintani, Aubrey and Donnellan (2016) revealed that a pre-task metalinguistic explanation about the past counterfactual conditional structure was superior to a post-task explanation in terms of the accurate written production of the target structure. They argued that the pre-task condition facilitated learners' on-task use of metalinguistic knowledge to monitor and revise their text, which is similar to the actual writing process. And, in a recent study, Sadeghi and Pourhaji (2021) found that providing explicit instruction prior to a focused story-retelling task negatively impacted fluent speech, yet enhanced global complexity and the rate and accuracy of relativization. Pre-task modeling as a pre-task FonF option was studied by Van de Guchte, Rijlaarsdam, Braaksma, and Bimmel (2017). Ninth-grade L2 German learners at a Dutch school watched two videos during which they either wrote sentences about the locations of the objects (the language-focused group) or responded to questions about the scenario (the meaning-oriented group). The target structure was German locative prepositions. After watching the videos, learners planned for 10 minutes prior to enacting a picture description task. It was found that the language-focused group performed significantly better than the meaning-focused group with regard to both attempted and accurate use of the target structure, yet the meaning-focused group demonstrated better syntactic complexity.

It should be acknowledged that the results of the pre-task FonF studies are very mixed, which makes it difficult to arrive at definite conclusions. Although some studies provide evidence that it can induce attempted and more accurate use of the targeted structure, others pinpoint the failure of pre-task instruction in directing learners' attention towards target structure use in their L2 productions. Furthermore, the extent to which the focus on the target structure in the pre-task stage influences general dimensions of language production remains unclear. Thus, there is obviously a need for more research to explore the impacts of explicit instruction on the performance of a focused task in different educational contexts and with different groups of learners and target linguistic features.

FonF in the during-task stage

The during-task stage, or the task cycle in Willis's (1996) model, refers to the learners' first performance of the task followed by a planning and reporting stage. Willis has firmly argued against a FonF during the task performance. She believes that during the performance of the task, learners need to focus on successful task completion and fluency development, not on accuracy (Willis, 1996). In addition, she asserts that learners are expected to utilize their own linguistic resources with the teacher offering assistance only when needed and does not attend to lexical or grammatical accuracy. The second part of the task cycle includes learners' planning their report of the way they completed the task followed by their report of it to the class by means of a written or oral presentation. Willis (1996) mentions that during the planning phase, prior to the public presentation, learners may also focus on accuracy by going through words and phrases they have doubts about.

Samuda (2001) expresses her concerns about Willis's proposal for advocating a sole focus on grammar when the task has already been carried out. She reasons that "certain aspects of certain forms may escape focus altogether if not in some way highlighted in task input, or nudged in task performance" (p. 122). Regardless of the provision or lack of any prior explicit instruction, opportunities arise to focus learners' attention on form—both implicitly and explicitly—during the performance of a task (Li *et al.*, 2016). In contrast to Willis, Long (2007) considers focus on form mainly as a during-task option. Long notes that such a FonF would be particularly successful since the linguistic focus is related to a meaning problem. Therefore, new form-meaning relationships are developed not through abstract language rules but by incidental learning which would be noticed instantly (Long, 2015). Long (2007, 2015) advises that the provision of negative corrective feedback to learners in the form of recasts is an ideal way of concisely attracting their attention to form. In the case of recasts, the interlocutor repeats the error back to the learner in a corrected form. Recasts fit easily in Long's conceptualization of FonF since the teacher responds immediately to the learner's error in the target language, while maintaining the focus on the meaning. In fact, a fundamental assumption of TBLT is that, although purely implicit learning is possible, attracting attention to form–meaning mappings would assist learning and, with respect to fragile grammatical structure(s) where the first language has an obstructive influence, may be crucial (Li *et al.*, 2016). It is this principle that lies beneath the significance that Long (1991) ascribed to FonF in TBLT. Primarily, FonF was closely related to the interaction hypothesis (Long, 1996), based on which the communication problems that learners encounter when they carry out tasks stimulate the negotiation of meaning, providing learners with input and pushing them to modify their output and thereby enhancing form–function mapping. Subsequently, scholars such as Lyster (e.g., Lyster, 2001), declared that FonF should not be restricted to occasions when communication problems happen but can be intentionally planned whenever a linguistic problem arises in what has become known as negotiation of form. Inducing a purposeful attention to form sits easily with focused tasks that are designed to obtain the use of a predetermined linguistic structure (Khezrlou, 2019a; Li *et al.*, 2016).

Besides Long's conversational FonF, Ellis *et al.* (2002) also postulate that learners may be corrected even if there is no problem in communication. The teacher may comprehend the learner's production, but still intends to direct the learner's attention to the error by correcting it. Ellis *et al.* (2002) describe this change in attention a "didactic" FonF maintaining that it pursues the goal of negotiating form instead of meaning during which learners are provided with feedback, varying from more implicit type of feedback such as requests for clarification or recasts to more explicit types. Explicit feedback can take the form of explicit correction in which learners are told, for example, "not goed, but went." There is also the metalinguistic corrective feedback which falls within the explicit category since it directly corrects the error by providing explanations, for example "you should use the past perfect here, not the simple past." Moreover, the teacher could intend to obtain the answer again in the hope that the learner will do it right, for instance by saying "let's try again" (for more examples of corrective feedback see Lyster and Ranta, 1997).

Ellis *et al.* (2002) underline the benefits of using more explicit types of corrective feedback in terms of the higher chances of noticeability of linguistic target structures they are correcting. With regard to recasts, learners may not always be conscious of their errors because they are not told that they have made a mistake or what the mistake was. Meta-analyses by Li (2010) and Lyster and Saito (2013) demonstrate that both implicit and explicit feedback types are beneficial to SLA. Furthermore, Lyster and Saito (2013) reported that the impacts were larger for the more explicit prompts compared to the implicit recasts. The significant effectiveness of TSLT which included explicit instruction particularly when it was also followed by within-task feedback was attested in Li *et al.*'s (2016) study. The study was conducted with eighth-grade Chinese learners aiming to facilitate the explicit and automated knowledge of past passive in an EFL context. The task-supported condition with the availability of corrective recast during the performance of a focused dictogloss task showed a consistent superiority over the explicit instruction without feedback, task only group, and feedback only group. Nevertheless, these effects were largely limited to the development of explicit knowledge as none of the groups outperformed the control group on the elicited imitation test.

FonF in the post-task stage

In the post-task phase, or what Willis (1996) calls language focus, learners examine specific features of the performance using their reports or transcripts. This is the position favored by some teachers and teacher educators due to the fact that attending to linguistic features during the performance of a task—either preemptively or reactively—would interfere with the main goal of a task which is to promote communicative confidence and fluency. Consequently, some teacher guides (e.g., Hedge, 2000) recommend that teachers monitor their learners carrying out tasks, make notes about any linguistic problems they show, and then attend to these explicitly when the task is completed. However, the study by Basturkmen, Loewen and Ellis (2004) revealed that the teachers they observed did not follow such advice and they unmindfully practiced focusing on form while the tasks were performed. SLA theories indicate the beneficial role of immediate FonF because of directing learners to notice linguistic features in a context where these forms are of communicative importance to them and to perform the cognitive comparisons that lead to modification in the interlanguage (Doughty, 2001). Transfer-appropriate processing also validates immediate rather than delayed FonF. Drawing on this theory, Lightbown (2008) argue that "we can use what we have learned if the cognitive processes that are active during learning are similar to those that are active during retrieval" (p. 27) and that there is a high likelihood that learners transfer what they have learned if FonF is integrated into an ongoing communicative activity instead of taking place in isolation as is the case when it is delayed. In contrast to these commentators and presuming that the development of accuracy is followed by that of fluency, Willis (1996) suggests that the post-task phase is the most appropriate stage for the integration of a focus on linguistic form and use. Willis argues that learners have already processed language for meaning in the task cycle and may then be asked to focus on particular linguistic features in the post-task in order to promote L2 learning. The activities learners may perform, consist of both analysis and practice activities, such as reflection on linguistic features, recycling of the task language, rechecking their text or audio or video or audio recording, or practicing useful phrases

(Willis, 1996). Ellis (2003, pp. 258–262) proposes three choices for a FonF in the post-task:

1) Learners can repeat the same or a similar task. Research has indicated that task repetition may enhance learners' both oral performance in terms of complexity, accuracy, and fluency (CAF) (Ahmadian & Tavakoli, 2011; Bygate, 1996, 2001; Gass *et al.*, 1999; Lambert *et al.*, 2017; Lynch & McLean, 2000, 2001) as well as their written performance (Amiryousefi, 2016; Fukunaga, 2021; Khezrlou, 2020a, 2021e; Kim *et al.*, 2020; Kim *et al.*, 2021; Lázaro-Ibarrola & Hidalgo, 2021);
2) Learners may reflect on how they performed their task; or
3) Learners may focus on linguistic forms that appeared to challenge them during the performance of the main task by reviewing errors, performing consciousness raising tasks, or production-practice and noticing activities.

In addition to these options which enhance consolidation and reflection, Skehan (1996, 1998) contends that the use of post-tasks might alter the way a task is performed and how attention is dedicated during the task. For instance, when learners are aware of the fact that they are required to present the outcome of their task to a public (Skehan & Foster, 1997) or transcribe their own previous task performance (Foster & Skehan, 2013; Qian, 2014) they may not only focus on a fluent but also a more accurate performance and may shift their attention from meaning to form in anticipation of a post-task activity.

Other researchers have employed more explicit FonF strategies that can be used effectively in the post-task. Three studies have explored the impacts of post-task metalinguistic explanation. Shintani and Ellis (2013), Shintani, Ellis, and Suzuki (2014) and Shintani (2017) provided L2 learners with a metalinguistic explanation handout immediately after a writing task and asked them to revise their text based on it. The results showed that the treatment led to a marked improvement in the accuracy in writing from the pretest to the posttest but resulted in a significant decrease in the delayed posttest. In one of my studies (Khezrlou, 2021a), Iranian EFL learners performed an oral narrative task after which they received explicit instruction of the English regular past tense structure. They then repeated the same task and lastly performed another oral narrative task with different content but same procedure. This study verified the efficacy of explicit instruction in leading to explicit and delayed implicit knowledge development. In another study, I (2021c) explored the impact of explicit instruction with different timing: (a) instruction before writing (pre-EI), instruction after writing (post-EI), and pre-writing explicit instruction also available during task performance (pre + online-EI). The results indicated that the pre + online-EI brought about higher accuracy in comparison to other conditions, with fluency developed only in the post-EI group.

Ellis's proposal for a modular curriculum

Ellis (2018, 2019a) proposes a modular language curriculum, involving a combination of task-based and task-supported language teaching (TBLT and TSLT, respectively). Given the SLA scholars' differing positions regarding the incompatibility and even the oppositional nature of TBLT and TSLT, Ellis's proposal is noteworthy. Ellis (2019a) states that when used in conjunction, TBLT and TSLT may have more benefits than either approach on its own, presenting two main justifications for this: the necessity of accuracy-based work to neutralize learned selective attention, and an identification of the less-than-ideal educational contexts where a lot of learners learn additional languages. In addition, he refers to two more issues supportive of his proposal. The first concerns the distinctions between individual learners' grammatical inferencing ability since some learners seem to learn complex grammatical structures through explicit instruction. The second issue pertains to the developmental variations between learners in terms of readiness to learn a particular structure. Naturally, a class of learners would comprise diverse aptitudes for grammatical inferencing and several developmental levels which lend support to Ellis's modular curriculum providing opportunities for both implicit and explicit learning.

The key question, then, becomes how to incorporate the TBLT and TSLT modules. Ellis (1993, 1994) drew on research in SLA to suggest a theory of instructed SLA favoring both a task-based and a structural syllabus. Ellis's theory is based on the difference between implicit and explicit knowledge and, specifically, on the role of explicit knowledge in the development of implicit knowledge. He supports an approach that starts with a task-based syllabus at lower levels of proficiency until learners use the language fluently, with the structural syllabus (i.e., TSLT) introduced at intermediate and advanced stages gradually. Ellis (1993) limits the role of a structural syllabus to the development of learners' explicit knowledge which he asserts could be accomplished through consciousness-raising tasks aimed at helping learners learn about linguistic features and later on facilitating the acquisition of implicit knowledge. He also offers two other options for combining structural and task-based syllabuses, which he prefers less. In the first, the structural and task-based components are introduced concurrently from the start to the end of the curriculum to develop explicit and implicit knowledge in parallel. And, in the second, the structural component precedes the task-based component to develop the learners' explicit knowledge prior to the introduction of the fluency-oriented component.

The third alternative endorsed by Ellis considers it vital to isolate the two syllabuses (e.g., taught on different days) (Ellis *et al.*, 2020). Ellis *et al.* (2020, p. 199) note that:

> The task-based syllabus is used to practice what is taught in the structural syllabus, the integrity of the task-based syllabus is compromised and the result is a task-supported syllabus rather than a modular syllabus. In this way, learners have the opportunity to access the full range of their own L2 resources to complete tasks.

To conclude, Ellis (2019a) argues that his modular curriculum materializes a realistic way to commence using TBLT in several international contexts. Hence, despite not making predictions of performance or the learning that occurs in the classroom, Ellis's modular syllabus design provides a more practical and feasible way of using tasks in many pedagogical contexts where teachers, learners and practitioners face challenges in moving away from the use of entirely structural syllabuses.

Conclusion

In this chapter, I have discussed numerous form-focused options available to teachers in the three phases of a task-based lesson to direct learners' attention to linguistic form. The place of FonF in TBLT is still a point of controversy among SLA researchers. Scholars vary in their arguments with some seeing no room for explicit instruction in the pre-task stage (e.g., Long and Willis), while others (DeKeyser and Skehan) supporting a pre-task attention to form, and yet others (Ellis) opting for a modular curriculum where the task-based component is primary and complemented by a structural component. Obviously, the educational contexts in some countries encourage form-focused lessons. Therefore, the suggestions for delaying FonF to the post-task stage often seems to be counterintuitive for teachers, particularly those who are used to the PPP approach. As Butler (2017) rightly notes, "in Asia, suggested modifications of TBLT often include form-focused instruction at the pre-task phase due to students' needs and other institutional requirements (e.g., requirement to cover prescribed vocabulary and grammatical items in the curriculum)" (p. 335). In these contexts, the teacher's role becomes vitally important, and as Van den Branden (2016, p. 167) overviews research on "the decisions and actions that teachers can (and according to some of these publications, should) take to optimally promote students' learning", these decisions and actions "may strongly differ from the prescriptions in the pedagogically oriented literature." As a result, the focal point is that a task-based syllabus has to be considered in relation to the context where it is implemented. Adaptations might be necessary in acquisition-poor settings and culturally challenging environments; nevertheless, in all contexts, it is important that the taskness of the activity should not be compromised.

6
Task Repetition

Introduction

TBLT researchers have closely investigated how tasks could be implemented in ways to maximize L2 development (Ellis, 2018) and the resulting benefits abound. One key task implementation condition which has attracted significant attention is task repetition (TR), which was first introduced by Bygate (1996, 2001). Bygate (2016) defined TR as the "repetition of the same or similar task" (p. 393). Research has generally demonstrated that repeating a task (or an aspect of a task) benefits learners' language output. Nevertheless, questions still remain as to how to make TR attractive and challenging for L2 learners so as to enhance their language learning without resulting in boredom and fatigue (Bygate, 2001). This chapter will first look at what it means to repeat oneself both in everyday life and in the context of language learning and why the latter is fruitful for the purpose of language development. Next, I overview the methodological aspects of TR. I then present the theoretical underpinnings for the TR and its benefits for better oral and written task performances. I conclude this chapter with a section on intervention in TR as an emerging line of research which has attracted much interest in recent years.

Why TR?

Language repeats itself in our everyday life (Larsen-Freeman, 2012). We repeat and re-use stock phrases and pleasantries such as "how you doing?" "chuffed to bits" "lovely weather." Of course, other ways of repeating things in our everyday lives might be reiterating a message to clarify it, or repeating things to hold them in memory such as when we practice a list of grocery items to purchase from the supermarket. Sometimes, we may practice a graduation speech several times in private. Therefore, practice is not just a part of everyday life, it is also a main factor included in language learning (DeKeyser, 2010; Lightbown, 2000) making it indispensable in L2 pedagogy. As Dekeyser (2010) and Larsen-Freeman (2012) noted, language teachers have long figured out the significance of practice in language teaching; nevertheless, the ways of using practice in the classroom has been a matter of much academic and pedagogic debate (DeKeyser, 2010, 2017). Perhaps, the first association that comes to mind when the word "practice" or "repetition" is used in relation to the language teaching setting is with audiolingual "drills" and pattern practice (Lynch & Maclean, 2000). In audiolingual drilling, the teacher gives a model which is then echoed by the whole class or by individual learners, as in the following example from Harmer (2001, pp. 79–80):

> Teacher: There's a cup on the table ... repeat
> Students: There's a cup on the table
> Teacher: Spoon
> Students: There's a spoon on the table
> Teacher: Book
> Students: There's a book on the table
> Teacher: On the chair
> Students: There's a book on the chair

This approach to "practice" is advocated by the behaviorist models of language learning which perceive language learning as the acquisition of 'behaviors' that could be fortified through positive reinforcement and rigorous repetition. Nonetheless, this approach to language learning is not deemed to be valid (Lightbown & Spada, 1999) with these types of drills being questioned for their value in language teaching since they do not teach the learners to engage in the language behavior of conceptualizing a meaning and articulating it through using the language, not to mention performing it in creative ways (DeKeyser, 2010). However, elements of this type of practice still exist in language classrooms under the guise of the "highly durable" (Ellis, 2003, p. 29) PPP method. Under that method, the teacher first presents the language to the learners followed by practicing it through controlled drills and role plays.

Finally, the learners show their understanding by producing spontaneous language in freer production activities (Westwood, 2016). DeKeyser (2010) contends that although repetition in the form of drills and pattern practice exercises do not benefit language learning, this does not denote that practice in any form should be discarded. As Larsen-Freeman (2012, p. 206) remarks, "(l)earning takes place not by repeating forms of a closed, static system, but by meaningfully playing the game while revisiting the same territory again and again." Thus, a purpose of language teaching is to enable learners to reenter the same territory continuously (Gatbonton & Segalowitz, 1988). One meaningful way of using practice in the classroom is task repetition, particularly considering the popularity and effectiveness of task-based or task-supported language teaching. TR does not require learners to repeat isolated words and phrases as in audiolingual drills; rather, it encourages them to engage and then re-engage in whole communicative sequences of linguistic performance.

TR in the field of TBLT has primarily gained prominence through the work of Bygate (1996, 2001, 2018; Samuda & Bygate, 2005). Bygate relies on Levelt's (1989) speech production model to frame his early proposals regarding the impacts of TR on L2 oral performance. Levelt's speech production consists of four interactive phases. The first step is conceptualization where the macro- and micro-planning of a message—planning of what one aims at expressing—is done, leading to a pre-verbal message. Formulation, the second stage, consists of the alteration of the pre-verbal message into linguistic form, depending on lexical, syntactic, and morpho-phonological encoding processes. When a speaker articulates the message at the third stage, phonological forms are actuated, and articulatory gestures are stimulated to produce the speech utterance. Lastly, monitoring takes place across all stages to ascertain that the evolving message is an accurate representation of the speaker's meaning and is formulated and articulated as intended. First language (L1) speakers carry out the formulation and articulation processes automatically, yet L2 speakers particularly at lower levels of linguistic proficiency face challenges in formulating their messages since they have a smaller L2 mental lexicon and have less complicated syntactic and morpho-phonological encoding skills. Therefore, in L2 speech, more arduous competition for attentional resources is expected to happen, leading to trade-off effects in the amount of attention learners have available for conceptualizing and formulating their message. Based on Levelt's (1989) model, Bygate (1996, 2001, 2018) suggested TR as a task condition that can relieve any trade-off effects that may occur between conceptualization and formulation processes during L2 speech production. As Bygate (2001) clarifies, some of the works of conceptualization, formulation and articulation that are performed in the first performance of a task may be held in the learners' memory store and can be reused in subsequent task performances. This may alleviate the pressure on learners' attentional capacity so that they would be able to attend to different aspects of their performance, especially formulation and articulation. This, in turn, is expected to manifest in positive developments in the syntactic complexity, accuracy, and/or fluency of L2 learners' performance.

Skehan's Limited Capacity model (LCM) also lends support to this line of reasoning which is also based on Levelt's speech production model to explicate task impacts. Skehan (1998, 2014) suggested that task features restrict the conceptualization and formulation operations, taxing learners' working memory resources with respect to different speech production stages. Skehan argues that more demanding tasks such as when a task includes unfamiliar information necessitate more attentional resources, thereby reducing learners' capacities to focus on both meaning and form. He suggests that manipulating task implementation conditions by using repeated task performances would alleviate pressure on both the conceptualizer and formulator and thus afford opportunities for learners to focus on both meaning and form. Hence, there will probably be lessened trade-off effects among the various CAF measures (Sample & Michel, 2014). Based on these arguments, Ellis (2003) asserted that TR might facilitate the restructuring of learners' interlanguage and that the enhancement in attentional resources may result in a renewed FonF. TR has also been considered to bring about an increase in procedural knowledge (DeKeyser, 1998) and automatization of language (de Jong & Perfetti, 2011). Indeed, findings from empirical works in TR have given general credence to the idea that repeated task performance can decline learners' cognitive load and enhance a FonF. Given the effectiveness of TR as a task implementation condition in L2 classroom, attention in both research and pedagogy has been directed to different types of TR and ways to enhance its effects on both oral and written task performances. In the remainder of this chapter, I will attend to each of these issues in detail.

Methodological aspects of task repetition

Type of repetition

Previous literature has operationalized TR in several different ways. In his doctoral research, Patanasorn (2010) specified three types of task repetition: 1) "task repetition" which consists of repetition of the exact same task; 2) "procedural repetition" which refers to the repetition of the same task procedure but with different content; and 3) "content repetition" in which the procedure changes yet the content or material remains the same. Indeed, Patanasorn's (2010) classification of TR is not entirely unambiguous or uncontroversial. Task repetition, for instance, refers to the repetition of the exact same task but this raises the question as to whether any subsequent task can ever be exactly the same since the task that has been performed previously means that the task demands are now diverse and the learner's approach to the task is likely to be different (Larsen-Freeman, 2009; 2012). Apart from this issue, the influence of a different day or time of day or all the other potential factors that might impact performance might mediate the impact of TR. There are also concerns regarding the pedagogic validity of repeating a task exactly (Ellis *et al.*, 2020). As we have seen, one of the purposes of TBLT is to motivate the use of tasks which have interactional authenticity, and therefore other types of TR such as procedural and content repetition might better fulfill this criterion.

Repetition of the type of task (procedural repetition) can also have numerous interpretations. Bygate (2001) mentioned that since familiarity with task type is considered to be stored in long-term memory, procedural repetition can release learners' attentional resources during task performance. Advocating this position, Fukuta (2016) states that familiarity with task content and/or its procedures can potentially enable learners' shift of attention to other dimensions of the target language, such as linguistic accuracy and lexical issues. In contrast to task repetition and procedural repetition, content repetition has not received much coverage in the literature. To my knowledge, only three studies have considered this approach to repetition (Carver & Kim, 2018; Garcia-Fuentes & McDonough, 2016; Patanasorn, 2010). Patanasorn (2010) is the primary attempt to compare different types of TR in terms of EFL learners' language development in classroom contexts. His findings revealed that the procedural repetition group performed significantly better in the accurate production of the simple past morphology, with the content repetition group outperforming in terms of fluency which, however, came at the expense of accuracy. Furthermore, exact task repetition alone did not result in fluency or accuracy enhancements. This finding was explained to result from the learners' failure in engaging with the iteration of identical tasks. It therefore remains to be seen how other researchers will interpret this type of repetition in their studies and what the findings will be. Carver and Kim's (2018) study examined the effectiveness of procedural and content repetition regarding learners' production of the French passé composé during task performance. It was found that although both TR types improved significantly from the pre-test to the post-test, the content repetition group supplied the target structure more frequently and accurately during task performance compared to the procedural repetition group. Thus, this study concluded that content familiarity with the same verbs had more of an influence on modifying learners' FonF than the procedural familiarity with different verbs.

A crucial question with respect to the characteristic of TR is whether different types of TR vary in their benefits for L2 learning. First, with regard to identical task repetition, the studies involving monologic tasks demonstrate that it improved CAF on the same task (Gass *et al.*, 1999; Bygate, 2001; Ahmadian & Tavakoli, 2011; Skehan *et al.*, 2012). Nevertheless, the effects fail to extend to new tasks (Gass *et al.*, 1999; Bygate, 2001). Concerning the studies that used group interaction, the findings underline the superiority of procedural repetition. In 2013, Kim conducted a partial replication of Patanasorn's (2010) study with 48 Korean EFL learners. She explored the way exact repetition and procedural repetition influenced the production and resolution of learners' attention to linguistic form during task performance. Attention to language form was operationalized as language-related episodes (LREs) (Swain & Lapkin, 1998). Kim found that procedural repetition led to more

LREs than the exact repetition, and as a result more opportunities for learning. Kim and Payant (2014) investigated the role of task complexity in addition to task repetition. Korean middle-school learners performed tasks in English under four conditions: simple tasks with both exact repetition and procedural repetition, and complex tasks with exact repetition and procedural repetition. They reported no effects for task-complexity on grammatical or lexical LREs but the exact repetition had a significant impact on both grammatical and lexical LREs. It was also observed that LREs in the procedural repetition condition increased over time regardless of task complexity, while LREs steadily declined over time in the exact repetition condition. Given the different methodological choices and the existence of multiple learner factors in these studies, it is recommended to have more work in this area with different populations, target features, and target languages. Second, studies that investigated procedural repetition indicated its effectiveness in bringing about an improvement in ratings of the performance of a new task (Gass *et al.*, 1999), improved accuracy in the English past tense (Patanasorn, 2010; Kim & Tracy-Ventura, 2013) and improved linguistic complexity (Kim & Tracy-Ventura, 2013). Lastly, content repetition led to improved global fluency but reduced accuracy in the past tense (Patanasorn, 2010). In sum, literature calls for the study of TR conditions particularly content repetition as an under-researched TR type and differing procedures in order to learn more about the role of repeating different aspects of tasks.

Number of repetitions

One other methodological aspect of TR worth mentioning here pertains to the number of repetitions. L2 learners have been asked to repeat their performance once (e.g., Ahmadian & Tavakoli, 2011; Bygate, 1996, 1999, 2001; Skehan *et al.*, 2012; Wang, 2014) or several times, with the number of times ranging from three or four (Gass *et al.*, 1999; Kim & Tracy-Ventura, 2013) to 11 (Ahmadian, 2011). Based on the results of these studies, performing tasks multiple times within a relatively short time interval is beneficial to the enhancement of learners' linguistic processing capabilities. However, it should be noted that the majority of empirical work has solely explored learners' performance over a small number of task repetitions (for exceptions, see Ahmadian, 2011, Lambert *et al.*, 2017; Lynch & Maclean, 2000, 2001). To date, the number of repetitions that can be sufficient for learners to advance the different aspects of their L2 production in the short term have not been the subject of adequate studies. Moreover, the number of repetitions might lead to different effects due to possible boredom and fatigue (Bygate, 2001). The study by Lambert *et al.* (2017) aimed at addressing different level Japanese English learners' language productions and reactions to performing three types of tasks (instruction, narration, and opinion) six times each within the time frame of a typical L2 lesson. They found that immediate same task repetition enhanced participants' oral fluency in all levels of proficiency and in all task types. Furthermore, gains in speech rate were the largest across the first three performances of each task type but continued until the fifth performance. And, regarding the perceptions of learners, a large number of participants highlighted the benefits of repetition in developing their fluency with only a few of them expressing fatigue in repeating the tasks six times with different partners. And, for those participants who considered the sixth time performance of a task needless, the optimal number of repetitions they perceived as being useful for the narration task was four, slightly less for the opinion task, and closer to three for the instruction task. To sum up, previous studies varied considerably in terms of the number of repetitions which indicate that it may be informative to compare different numbers of repetitions with the same interval on L2 development.

Interval of repetition

A second methodological variable is the interval of repetition. There is evidence in cognitive and educational psychology that the effects of repeated practice opportunities spaced by time or events (i.e., distributed practice) are more robust and reliable than repeated practice opportunities in immediate succession (i.e., massed practice) (for reviews see Carpenter, 2017 and Cepeda *et al.*, 2006). In SLA, skill acquisition theory sets out to account for "how people progress in learning a variety of skills, from initial learning to advanced proficiency" (DeKeyser, 2015, p. 94). Adaptive control of thought–rational model (ACT–R; Anderson, 1993) as the most widely accepted model of skill acquisition posits that the learning of different skills goes through a similar path of development from primary representation of knowledge to highly skilled behaviors. In other words, skills are normally primarily learned as declarative knowledge (or knowledge about the grammatical rules). This initial learning is followed by a rapid stage of proceduralization (knowledge compilation), which results in qualitatively different procedural knowledge (or knowledge about how to use the rules) through initial practice. Procedural knowledge can be automatized over a long period of time with further extensive practice (Anderson, 1993; DeKeyser, 2015). When it comes to optimal spacing of practice for proceduralization/automatization of L2 skills, studies have yielded conflicting results, with some demonstrating benefits for spacing longer than 2-3 days (e.g., Bird, 2010; Rogers, 2015), and others finding benefits for spacing shorter than seven days (e.g., Suzuki, 2017; Suzuki & DeKeyser, 2017).

In TR research, in addition to immediate repetition (e.g., de Jong & Perfetti, 2011; Lambert *et al*., 2017; Lynch & Maclean, 2000; Thai & Boers, 2016), other intervals include one day (Kim & Tracy-Ventura, 2013), two to three days (Ahmadian & Tavakoli, 2011; Gass *et al*., 1999), weeks (Fukuta, 2016; Hsu, 2017) and fortnightly (Azkarai & Garcia Mayo, 2016; Bygate, 2001). What these studies have demonstrated is that fluency is boosted by TR irrespective of the interval between the original and subsequent performance(s). This means that fluency is relatively strongly impacted by TR. These conclusions, however, are not clearly upheld for accuracy and complexity. Generally, it seems that a short interval between the main and following task performance enhances the possibility of an effect for accuracy and complexity. Bui *et al*. (2019) provide an explanation that if the repetition intervals are very short (i.e., immediately after the first task performance), L2 learners would be more likely to draw on recently activated and retrieved lemmas which would enhance the speed of processing. This position receives support from de Jong's (2012) argument that "immediate repetition makes it more likely that benefits of conceptualization and formulation persist into the repeated deliveries" (de Jong, 2012, p. 44). Consequently, it appears that if particular language production processes are accelerated by recency of use, then more attentional capacities would become available for monitoring processes. This could in turn enhance complexity and accuracy. Nevertheless, accuracy and complexity might not be impacted to the same extent as fluency (Skehan, 1998, 2014, 2018a). Previous studies have reported that for complexity and accuracy to develop from the main to the following task performance, some time needs to be provided to the learners in order to facilitate their storage of the new form-meaning pairings in long-term memory. This will then be followed by the conscious or unconscious comparison of form-meaning mappings against the target-like forms that the learners have in their declarative memory or with those that they may encounter in the input (see Housen *et al.*, 2012). On these grounds, then, it could be supposed that relatively longer time intervals (such as a few days) between the two task performances may make learners to be less fluent/more cautious, but more accurate/complex since they have had masses of time to process the task content and check the accuracy of form-function mappings consciously (Bui *et al.*, 2019). This would in turn stimulate them to self-monitor and self-correct their language which could lead them to become more accurate/complex but less fluent (Kormos, 2006).

These speculations are advocated by Lambert *et al.*'s (2017) findings and also explain why impacts on accuracy and complexity are often only seen on the third performance (e.g., Boers 2014; Thai & Boers, 2016). To the best of my knowledge, Bui *et al.*'s (2019) study has been the only attempt in search of optimal spacing of practice for different levels of long-term retention. In their study, EFL learners in Hong Kong engaged in oral picture description tasks twice under five different schedules (0-day [massed], 1-day, 3-day, 7-day, and 14-day intervals). Their findings indicated that although spacing between repeated task performances did not have major impacts on all measures of performance, the effects of TR on some complexity and fluency measures were mediated by the length of interval. More specifically, speech rate increased when the interval between the two performances was very short (immediate), yet structural complexity and some repair measures developed when there was a one-week interval. Also, accuracy was not found to be related to the spacing between performances. Bui *et al.* suggest that "a combination of tasks which include some immediate repetition and those with a weekly interval can help contribute to the improvement of L2 performance" (p. 26). Bui *et al.*'s study is a good starting point to see how intervals of repetition can be manipulated to promote L2 development. However, the small sample size in their study and the limited proficiency of participants which challenged them to make significant improvements in a few days or weeks regarding accuracy necessitate more replication studies in this area.

TR in speaking and writing

The majority of studies on TR reviewed in this chapter investigated repeated effects on L2 speech production and largely overlooked the impacts on L2 writing. Although the linguistic processes learners use while involved in spoken and written production are largely similar (Kellogg, 1996), the distinct nature of written communication deserves particular attention. As touched on earlier in this chapter, Levelt (1989) outlined four important stages in speech production: conceptualization, formulation, articulation, and self-monitoring. Kellogg's (1996) model of writing processes is comparable to Levelt's (1989) model since it explains how writers engage in writing processes consisting of formulation, execution, and monitoring. Formulation involves two sub-processes of planning and translation. Planning entails thinking up ideas to organize the content. Translating involves activating semantic, syntactic, phonological, and orthographic sub-processes to select lexical units, build a syntactic frame, phonologically represent the lexical units in the frame, and convert phonemes into graphemes. Execution is the actual production of the written words, phrases, and sentences. Lastly, monitoring encompasses reading and editing the already written text to find problems and fix them. Kellogg's (1996) model posits that these three writing processes function consecutively, but parallel processing might take place in writing when processing demands do not overload working memory. Clearly, although both Levelt's and Kellogg's models represent the processes involved in language production which are largely similar with respect to planning the content, encoding linguistic forms, execution, and monitoring, they are distinct since the modes of production are different (Kormos, 2014). Considering the linear nature of speaking limited by real-time pressure, L2 speakers commonly become involved in conceptualizing, formulating, and monitoring successively, while writing is a revisionary process carried out under less real-time pressure;

therefore, L2 writers can proceed with idea planning, linguistic encoding, and textual revising recursively (Abdi Tabari, 2021). Additionally, compared to speaking, writing allows for more opportunities for editing mental and textual representation outputs during planning and production (Manchón, 2014). Ellis and Yuan (2005, p.175) offer another difference between speech and writing. That is, unlike speech, the result of writing is a "visual object (the written message), which is amenable to inspection in a way that the aural trace left by a spoken message is not." Ellis and Yuan believe that this makes mistakes clear and as a result facilitates monitoring. Lastly, L2 writers usually obtain written corrective feedback (WCF) on their written texts and are able to go back over their writing, or over the feedback received which, in theory, allows them to be more in control of their attentional resources, and more likely to prioritize linguistic concerns and attend to language (Manchón, 2014). These differences between speaking and writing, hence, could have diverse effects on the effects of TR leading to different outcomes in L2 production.

So far, a few studies have investigated the effects of TR on L2 writing. The few writing TR studies available (Amiryousefi, 2016; Nitta & Baba, 2014, 2018; Sánchez et al., 2020) once again empirically verify the language learning benefits resulting from repeating a writing task. Both Nitta and Baba (2014) and Amiryousefi (2016) found gains in fluency, with Nitta and Baba (2014) reporting the effectiveness of TR in leading to greater complexity in the long term at the expense of the initial enhancements in fluency (Nitta & Baba, 2018). Amiryousefi's (2016) study revealed higher accuracy resulting from TR although complexity was not developed. Sánchez et al. (2020) looked into the effects of TR in speaking and writing in one single study. Twenty-nine Spanish EFL participants individually performed a decision-making task in speaking or in writing. Eight days after the first performance, they were asked to repeat the same task in the same modality. It was found that repeating tasks in speaking or writing by higher and lower L2 proficiency learners did not positively influence lexical complexity and accuracy and even negatively affected syntactic complexity. There were however some modality-related effects such that writing elicited more complex language in terms of one dimension of syntactic complexity (noun phrase complexity) and lexical complexity (lexical richness, lexical variety and lexical sophistication), although this last effect was mediated by proficiency. Sánchez et al. explain that "as the higher proficiency writers in our study had more linguistic resources at their disposal than their lower-proficiency counterparts, and given the greater availability of time while writing, they seemed to have set more complex linguistic goals and, consequently, only these learners were able to deploy a more varied, rich, and sophisticated language" (p. 136). These results give partial credence to Manchón's (2014) prediction that the second performance of a writing task can complexify goals. Additionally, the high proficiency learners' attention to use of lexis across repeated tasks was explained from the perspective of the main role of lexical use and lexical searches in writing. Lastly, Sánchez et al. reported modality-related TR effects in speaking fluency, an effect observed in the oral mode but not in writing.

Sánchez et al.'s (2020) study was one of the first to explore the role that mode of production plays in the effectiveness of TR. The results were promising in illuminating the task-modality effects. One finding of this study worth mentioning here is the observed lack of positive effects of TR on low proficiency participants' L2 production in any of the CAF measures used. This result brings to the fore the argument that for TR in writing to lead to enhanced performance with low proficiency L2 users, either massed repetition (Nitta & Baba, 2014) or a combination of TR with some sort of external form-focused intervention such as WCF in between repeated task performances (Ellis, 2009a, 2019b; Manchón, 2014) is needed. The intervention issue has led to a batch of studies in recent years investigating the role of form-focused intervention in TR which I will turn to in the next section.

Form-focused intervention in TR

A general finding of the bulk of the TR studies to date has been that "task repetition benefits fluency and sometimes complexity but is less likely to lead to gains in global accuracy" (Sheppard & Ellis, 2018, p. 175). This is attributed by Ellis (2009a) to the lack of a FonF intervention between repeated task performances to reinforce learners' attention to form. Thus, Ellis (2009a, 2019b) encourages the use of a form-focused intervention technique between repeated task performances to transfer the positive impacts of TR to a new task, ending in language learning. A limited yet growing number of studies in recent years have begun to examine the role of intervention in TR. Probably the first study carried out on the effectiveness of intervention in TR was that of Sheppard (2006). He provided input and feedback between repeated oral tasks which contributed to the development of all performance dimensions of CAF in both the repeated and new tasks. More recently, Sheppard and Ellis (2018) attempted to engage learners in a stimulated recall procedure after their first oral narrative task performance and found that both the stimulated recall group and the task repetition only group fostered their fluency in the repeated tasks, but not in the new task. Besides, complexity and accuracy remained unchanged over time. Contrary to Sheppard and Ellis's findings, Fukuta's (2016) study indicated remarkable enhancements in oral accuracy but not fluency and complexity in the repeated task performance following a stimulated recall procedure. The different effects for the stimulated recall intervention on accuracy in these two studies might be ascribed to participants' proficiency levels (upper-intermediate in Fukuta's study and beginner in Sheppard and Ellis's study) and the spacing between task repetitions (a one-week interval in Fukuta's study and an immediate repetition followed by a second repetition and a new task performance two weeks after the first repetition in Sheppard and Ellis's study). Additionally, the focus of stimulated recall in these two studies differed.

Adopting a different intervention technique, van de Guchte et al. (2016) offered corrective feedback to Dutch EFL learners' main task performance followed by the repetition of a similar task. Results verified the effectiveness of this intervention strategy in learners' acquisition of two German grammar structures. Kartchava and Nassaji (2019) asked intermediate learners to prepare and deliver a technology-based oral presentation. While the experimental group learners reflected on their performance and received feedback from the teacher prior to their repeated performance, the control group learners enacted the task once with no feedback. Predictably, task repetition along with learners' reflection resulted in overall effective task performance. In another study, Khezrlou (2019b) investigated task repetition and procedural repetition both preceded by two types of oral corrective feedback: clarification request and recast. Findings confirmed that the saliency offered by the clarification request compared to the recast enhanced learners' accuracy in the repeated performance and the new task performance in the long run. Lastly, Khezrlou (2021a) underlined the role of explicit instruction between the same oral narrative tasks in fostering learners' immediate and delayed explicit knowledge development and the development of delayed implicit knowledge. Overall, results of TR studies in the oral domain with a pedagogic intervention confirm the important role of a FonF technique in effectively attracting learners' attention to form.

Intervention studies in the realm of repeated writing tasks have been mostly centered on the effects of WCF. Kim *et al.* (2020) investigated whether the provision of indirect synchronous WCF could mediate the TR effects. They found that whereas TR without feedback cultivated writing fluency, TR with synchronous feedback negatively influenced fluency during collaborative writing but it was successful in increasing accuracy in learners' writing. Khezrlou (2020a) demonstrated that when learners received reformulation feedback between repeated performances of the same written narrative task (TR+R), they produced more complex language in terms of subordination in the immediate terms than the group that received error correction between repeated performances (TR+EC) or the control TR group. And, although the TR+EC learners carried over their enhanced accuracy from the repeated task to new task performances, only the TR+R and TR groups generated fluent productions. I explained that these results could be due to Iranian EFL learners' familiarity with explicit methods of correction compared to reformulation as an unfamiliar feedback type to most learners. Amelohina *et al.* (2020) explored the effects of exact task repetition and procedural task repetition along with direct and indirect WCF. Results revealed progression towards more accurate, fluent, and, in part, complex performance and the direct WCF was more effective than the less explicit indirect WCF. Corroborating Amelohina *et al.*'s findings, Khezrlou's (2021e) study investigated the effects of TR with metalinguistic feedback, direct feedback, or mixed direct metalinguistic feedback on learners' explicit knowledge, automatized explicit knowledge, and written accuracy. It was found that the mixed feedback led to gains in explicit knowledge and written accuracy particularly for those learners with some prior knowledge of the structure. Nevertheless, there were no effects on automatized explicit knowledge in any of the TR conditions. In sum, the results of these studies attest Manchón's (2014) suggestion that the provision of WCF is likely to prompt learners to focus on form during the second performance of the task, which may lead at least to increased accuracy. However, the infancy of this research area as well as the remarkable methodological variations in the literature necessitate the conduction of more studies with different types of intervention strategies in both speaking and writing domains.

Conclusion

I would like to close this chapter with some empirical and methodological conclusions. In essence, TR is a task implementation option, which, as Skehan (2014) has stressed, compared to the task design option, has more effect on achieving a balanced task performance in terms of CAF. Task implementation options including TR also have more pedagogical importance since "they can be easily acted on by teachers" (Ellis, 2019b, p. 17). Given the empirical evidence largely in support of task repetition in fostering L2 development, TR is suggested as a beneficial implementation choice in enhancing fluency and complexity— particularly if the task is repeated multiple times. And, in order to gain the benefits of TR on accuracy, there would be a need for some extra form-focused intervention. As Skehan (2014) underlines, TR is an effective pedagogic choice, yet an overview of the recent research indicates that the full value of TR may only be realized if it is combined with some other implementation option (Ellis, 2019b). Clearly, we need to know what role the language-related, task-related, feedback-related, and learner-related factors play in bringing about learning via repeating tasks. It is hoped that the pedagogical and empirical insights provided in this chapter can encourage the practice of TR in language classrooms and inform future research in the domain.

7
Task Planning

Introduction

Planning, or the provision of preparation time prior to the performance of a task, is one of the pedagogic options most widely used in language classrooms and researched in the TBLT literature (see Ellis, 2019b). The justification for task planning is that if learners are asked to plan, their limited attentional resources are alleviated during actual task performance and as a result more space becomes available for focusing on micro aspects of production in addition to content and meaning, including the formal dimensions of the L2 code. Within the TBLT framework, task planning has been operationalized in different forms such as strategic planning and online planning which are considered as a means of promoting learners' preparedness for task performance (Ellis, 2019). Task planning has been primarily measured in relation to CAF (Housen *et al*., 2012) and the results of planning studies have demonstrated that pre-task planning helps learners organize their conceptual plans and utilize their attentional resources, thereby generating more fluent and complex language, although it does not necessarily improve accuracy. These consistent findings regarding the impacts of task planning on L2 production have encouraged the movement of the TBLT literature beyond a Black Box approach to thinking about planning (Skehan, 2018b). We are now in a position to move forward and see how we can ensure the reality of transfer from planning to task performance. Relevant issues in this chapter will be the importance of planning, types of task planning, the planning mechanisms, and the trainability of planning.

The nature of planning

From an information processing framework, planning is considered as a problem-solving operation (Newell & Simon, 1972). It is a mental procedure consisting of objective setting, problem prediction, information collection and organization, and strategy development for the aim of conducting a particular task (Simon, 1978). Accordingly, planning is a process individuals naturally engage in when they aim at solving a problem. In the realm of language learning, planning was conventionally perceived as an equivalent of monitoring (Krashen, 1981). It is generally related to language production yet the processes involved in it are not precisely the same in diverse settings. In studies attending to the process of speech production (e.g., Levelt, 1989), planning is distinguished from monitoring and solely alludes to the process of retrieving and organizing information before an utterance is produced. In these studies, monitoring is viewed as a process of reviewing and editing which happens during articulation (e.g., Butterworth, 1980). Wendel (1997) argued that planning and monitoring are both activities that occur at the central processing stage of information processing and can potentially influence output. He retitled them as strategic planning (i.e., planning) and on-line planning (i.e., monitoring) with the former being conducted before language production while the latter taking place during actual production. In effect, Wendel's perspective of planning is similar to that of Levelt (1989) on the grounds that planning occurring before production is distinguished from the planning—monitoring—which happens during production. Different from oral language production, in written production, planning is not differentiated from monitoring and has been referred to as a more common term that encompasses both preparation for language use and the action of task completion. Hayes and Nash (1996) define planning as "the combination of the goal and the sequence of steps to achieve that goal" (p. 32) including two stages. The first stage entails representing the preferred outcome or purpose of the task and examining the resources available for performing the task. The second stage refers to the actual performance of the task, during which different purposes and methods are attempted until a satisfactory correspondence between the objective and means for achieving it is discovered. Hayes and

Nash (1996) state that the relationship between planning and an action of task completion is that planning directs action but does not control it. It provides recommendations for action and alters them as action progresses. In writing, a differentiation is made between process planning and text planning (Hayes & Nash, 1996). Process planning refers to the ways or strategies the writer identifies for performing the writing task whereas text planning refers to the text being written. In text planning, two types of planning are further identified: abstract text planning and language planning. Abstract text planning occurs when writers get involved in idea generation and conceptual planning without determining the language to be produced. In language planning, on the other hand, writers plan for the specific words and sentences to be utilized. The relationship between abstract text planning and language planning is very close making it challenging to make a difference between the two. Both process planning and text planning are activities that are entailed in what will be called pre-task planning, which I will explain in the following section. Text planning will be the principal activity included in what will be called online planning (see next section for a discussion).

Types of planning

In 2005, Ellis recommended a way to classify planning based on its timing—either before a task is enacted or during the performance of a task. Thus, the former type of planning is termed pre-task planning and the latter within-task planning. In the following section, I will describe each type of planning along with the results of research on their roles in L2 production.

Pre-task planning

Pre-task planning is itself categorized into rehearsal and strategic planning (Ellis, 2005). Rehearsal refers to task repetition in which learners are provided with opportunities to carry out a task more than once and the first performance serves as a preparation for a subsequent performance (see Chapter 6). Strategic planning refers to the pre-task activity in which learners make a strategic plan for the task and plan the content and language essential for task completion without practicing the task before its performance. During strategic planning learners are generally presented with the task and they are encouraged to activate their schemata and language resources in order to prepare for the task. In the strategic planning condition, learners may practice the content and language for the task. Nevertheless, they usually cannot rehearse the task completely considering that the provided time is only adequate for developing a strategic plan. Although both rehearsal and strategic planning are entailed in pre-task planning, the majority of previous studies on planning (e.g., Crookes, 1989; Foster & Skehan, 1996; Kawauchi, 2005; Mehnert, 1998; Ortega, 1999, 2005; Skehan & Foster, 1997, 2005; Wendel, 1997; Wigglesworth, 1997; Yuan & Ellis, 2003) used the term pre-task planning to refer to strategic planning only. Being one of the first attempts to explore the effectiveness of pre-task planning, Crookes's (1989) study examined Japanese learners' oral task performance when they were either provided with a ten-minute preparation time or they did not receive any such opportunity. The study revealed that planning affected complexity in terms of lexical variety and syntactic complexity measured by words per utterance, subordination and S-nodes per utterance; however, there were no differences with respect to general accuracy measured through the number of error-free T-units. Ellis (2009b) synthesized the studies conducted on the role of pre-task planning in task performance in terms of CAF of learners' speech production, highlighting the consistent efficacy of planning on fluency and complexity yet inconclusive impacts on accuracy. Ortega (1999) also reported mixed findings with regard to the role of pre-task planning in accuracy, contending the difficulty of observing any consistent pattern of results of planning studies in terms of accuracy.

Naturally, the question arises here as to why pre-task planning has notable impacts on complexity and fluency than accuracy. The principal justification appears to be the learners' devotion of most of their planning time to the configuration of the content instead of the language of their task performance, which releases the pressure on the conceptualizer and results in more fluent and complex language (Ellis *et al.*, 2020). This speculation is in line with Sangarun (2005) who found that learners' planning was mainly focused on meaning irrespective of whether they focused on language or content. Ellis *et al.* (2020) further clarify that "during task performance, learners must match the planned content with the relevant linguistic items, leading to more complex language. The elevated complexity is probably obtained at the expense of accuracy, confirming Skehan's LAC" (p. 213).

Theoretically, task planning has been widely related to the predictions of Skehan's LAC (Skehan, 2014, 2016; Skehan & Foster, 2001) which hypothesizes that L2 learners have a limited processing capacity and face difficulty in devoting their full attention to both meaning and form at the same time; consequently, they have to select between the two and typically prioritize meaning over form. LAC posits that the pre-task planning may mitigate the cognitive load of tasks requiring L2 learners to allocate more attentional resources to the production of higher linguistic quality. The findings of planning research have often been mentioned to give credence to Skehan's theory and oppose Robinson's cognition hypothesis (see Chapter 5), which does not consider a trade-off between complexity and accuracy since they draw on distinct resources, and that learners' task performance is influenced by the processing demands of the task, rather than the learners' limited attentional capacity. Pedagogically, some teachers value the allocation of pre-task planning time for learners to carry out their task smoothly and calmly. Others, on the other hand, believe that pre-task planning may incline learners towards not being able to communicate their message in spontaneous communication. An array of research examining pre-task planning, however, have produced results that offer some valuable pedagogical implications for L2 teachers who would like to help their learners perform their tasks efficiently. One line of inquiry within the pre-task planning literature has attended to the appropriate length of planning time on the performance of learners (see Li *et al.*, 2015). Li *et al.* (2015) reported that too short a time (e.g., 30 seconds) and too long a time (e.g., five minutes) deteriorated the effectiveness of planning with one-three minutes for planning being the most effective length that can lead to significant improvements in speech production in terms of CAF and most considerably in accuracy. As Li *et al.* clarify, longer planning time such as 10 minutes which has been set as the default time in most planning research does not necessarily bring about enhanced performance, "with the effects of planning duration being non-linear, with shorter planning times showing larger effects" (Ellis *et al.*,

2020, p. 215). Also, in classroom contexts which impose time restrictions on teachers' pedagogical practices, giving more than five minutes for pre-task planning does not seem feasible. However, it should be noted that it is the teachers who implement the tasks in the classroom and are therefore in better positions to figure out the most effective length of planning that works for their learners and specific instructional context based on the type, complexity, and purpose of the task.

Another area of study within the pre-task planning literature has been the investigation of the monologic and dialogic tasks. Whereas the earlier studies looked into the impacts of pre-task planning on interactive tasks, a large number of recent studies used monologic tasks (Aubrey *et al.*, 2020; Aubrey & Philpott, 2022; Bui, 2021; Chen, 2020; Kang & Lee, 2019; O'Grady, 2019; Qin & Zhang, 2019) with only a handful using interactive tasks (Gu, 2021; Hsu, 2012; Kim, 2013). Kim's (2013) study provided a task modeling for one group through watching a video in the 10-minute planning time while the other group was asked to plan individually for 10 minutes. Kim reported that watching the videos enabled learners to focus more on language in terms of question formation, through generating more language-related episodes (i.e., discussion of form) when they performed the interactive tasks and thus led to better development. In contrast to Kim's findings, however, neither Hsu nor Gu could find any benefits for pre-task planning in dialogic tasks. Hsu (2012) compared a group that had both time to plan and unpressured online planning and a group that received unpressured online planning yet with no opportunity to plan. Results did not indicate group differences in any of the CAF measures, which Hsu attributed to the learners' lack of familiarity with performing an interactive task in a chat environment. Gu (2021) investigated the role of pre-task planning and unpressured on-line planning in Chinese EFL learners' performance in an oral dialogic task condition. It was found that pre-task planning did not enhance L2 performance in all dimensions and led to a trade-off effect between complexity and accuracy. These results pinpointing the negative impacts of pre-task planning on L2 production—particularly on attention to form— might be explained by the fact that in interactive tasks, planning boosts learners' familiarity with the content and therefore declines the need for negotiation—a feature that is a key source of learning in view of the interactionists (Gass, 1997; Long, 1996; see Chapter 3).

Within-task planning

Within-task planning, as its name implies, refers to the planning activities that learners engage in during task performance. It is also referred to as online planning, which is defined as the formulating process (in terms of both content and language) and the monitoring of output (Yuan & Ellis, 2003) that a speaker or writer engages in during language production. Within-task planning is itself differentiated by two conditions: pressured and unpressured (Ellis, 2005). Under the pressured condition, learners are provided with a time limit to complete the task, making their on-line planning pressured by both time and communication needs. In contrast, unpressured within-task planning condition allows learners to take their time when performing the task so they can carefully plan their language on-line. The majority of previous research on online planning has operationalized it as the provision of unlimited time to the learners (e.g., Ellis & Yuan, 2004) or longer time than other groups of participants (e.g., Li, 2004) in order to release time pressure. The literature suggests that unpressured time conditions usually are associated with greater accuracy in learners' speech performance fairly consistently, and occasionally there are increases in structural complexity (Ahmadian & Tavakoli, 2011; Ellis & Yuan, 2005; Hsu, 2015; Yuan & Ellis, 2003). The interpretation is that supportive online conditions lead to better opportunities for monitoring and for speech formulation processes.

Nevertheless, Skehan and Foster (2005) underscored that it is only an assumption that learners would be involved in online planning when they complete tasks without time pressure and that this assumption cannot be confirmed until there is evidence on learners' behavior and mental mechanisms during task performance under an online planning condition. Regardless of the validity of Skehan and Foster's argument, there have been very few studies to examine learners' behaviors during the pre-task planning time (see the next section) and only one to focus on online-planning. Rostamian, Fazilatfar and Jabbari (2017) is probably the only endeavor to examine learners' cognitive processes during the online-planning time. In this study, Iranian EFL learners were asked to perform written narrative tasks under four planning conditions: (1) no planning (NP) in which the task was performed under time pressure, (2) online-planning (OLP) in which the task was conducted without time pressure, (3) pre-task planning (PTP) where learners performed the task after 10 minutes of pre-planning, and (4) pre-task and on-line planning (PTOLP) condition which provided a 10-minute pre-planning time along with the performance of the narrative task without time pressure. The learners' writing processes were videotaped for a following stimulated recall session. Results revealed that the OLP group had the most "proposing processes" to plan the ideas to be expressed and also went through more instances of translation by spending more time to find better lexical and grammatical correspondents and revision processes to evaluate their texts compared to the other groups. The comparison of the PTP group and the OLP group demonstrated the positive impact of on-line planning on accuracy and the effectiveness of pre-task planning on fluency and syntactic complexity. Rostamian *et al.* explained that the OLP provided learners with sufficient time to focus on translation combined with revising processes and thus led to a significant increase in accuracy at the expense of syntactic complexity. They concluded that both pre- and on-line planning improve performance: pre-planning reduces the pressure on planning the content, translating those plans into written text through selecting lexical items and the appropriate structure, and reviewing those written texts or plans at the time of writing that leads to more fluency and syntactic complexity; on-line planning pushes translating and reviewing processes to produce more accurate language.

The results of Rostamian *et al.*'s study signify the importance of not considering the pre-task planning and within-task planning as mutually exclusive of each other. The two types of planning can be manipulated by teachers/researchers and integrated in various ways, such as 1) pre-task planning with pressured within-task planning; 2) pre-task planning with unpressured within-task planning; 3) unpressured within-task planning; or 4) pre-task planning alone, etc. Both types of planning may ease the processing load of learners and promote language performance. Of equal importance is noting the impossibility of developing a pre-task planning condition where online planning is avoided or, vice versa, an online planning condition without pre-task planning. Even when learners are performing under time pressure they might still get involved in some online planning and when they are enacting a task without time pressure, they could spend a little time to do pre-task planning. This particularly holds true in the case of writing. As a result, the two types of planning should be regarded as relative terms. That is, a pre-task planning condition offers relatively more opportunities for learners to engage in pre-task planning and an online planning presents relatively more opportunities to engage in online planning. To sum up, research has provided evidence that within-task planning may assist with the formal features of task performance and also have a positive impact on learning. This might be especially true for beginner learners who may need more time to plan and monitor their task performance.

Planning processes

The impact of planning on task performance is largely based on what learners actually do during the time provided for their planning. A limited number of studies conducted in recent years have intended to examine what learners carry out during the pre-task planning time (Bui & Teng, 2018; Lee & Burch, 2017; Ortega, 2005; Pang & Skehan, 2014), shedding some light onto the planning strategies that learners use and how they contribute to successful task performance. In her two-study report, Ortega (2005) looked into the benefits afforded by pre-task planning through an exploration of what learners say they do when they plan. Based on an analysis of retrospective interviews, Ortega reported that learners mostly employed retrieval strategies (i.e., gaining access to ideas and language) and rehearsal strategies (i.e., practicing the performance) to prepare themselves for the speaking task. The study also found that lower proficiency learners frequently used retrieval strategies while higher proficiency learners used both rehearsal and retrieval. Although Ortega's study examined the strategies used by learners during planning time, it did not relate the used strategies to the success or failure of learners' task performance. Expanding on Ortega's (2005) study, Pang and Skehan (2014) investigated self-reported planning behaviors, but they also attempted to relate these findings to the following task performance. They analyzed the retrospective interview data in light of Levelt's (1989) model of speech production, which indicated the higher proficiency learners' reliance on the conceptualization stage of planning, while lower proficiency learners attended to formulation. The results of relation between planning and performance revealed that when learners focused on planning structure, realistic language, and specific content rather than general content, the quality of their speech in terms of CAF was improved. Based on these results, Pang and Skehan suggested the following operating principles for effective pre-task planning in L2 speech production:

- Build your own structure (the speaker needs to impose organization on what is to be said (e.g., *plan how to tell the story*, or *rehearse to check whether what is planned is logical and clear*)).
- Avoid trouble, and be realistic (the speaker uses planning time to prepare simpler things and to work within their limited abilities (e.g., *choose to use simple words*, or *rehearse*)).
- Handle trouble when it occurs (for example, when difficulties arise, the speaker needs to re-join the flow of ideas that the first principle provides. Therefore, they retrieve a parallel mode of processing rather than a serial mode. Other recommended strategies are *lexical compensation* and *circumlocution*).
- Plan small or specific versus plan general (the speaker needs to *plan small details such as a detailed description of the events in the story* rather than planning general things such as *describing the general plot of the story*).
- Avoid grammar focus (focus on grammar has no influence on accuracy and negatively impacts fluency and complexity; hence, speakers need to *have no or little concern about grammar use*).

Using retrospective interviews to explore learners' planning processes, Bui and Teng's (2018) recent study verified the planning behaviors reported in Ortega's and Pang and Skehan's studies. Interestingly, Bui and Teng also found affective influences of planning such that the planning time made numerous participants feel anxious towards the performance of the speaking task, which led to confidence issues and forgetting some of their planned lexical items during the performance. These confusion and anxiety feelings during the planning time is a further testament for the need to find out what learners do during the planning time and equip them with the right set of strategies.

The results related to planning behaviors addressed by the above studies indicate important patterns which need to be confirmed and extended. Such results mean that attention allocation can be manipulated, and that, within the limitations of the total amount of attention available, more than one performance area can be elevated. Pre-task conditions can impact form in performance, signifying that learners' attentional priorities can be manipulated through explicit training. Training planning is a new area of research in the task planning literature with the aim of helping learners use effective strategies in their pre-task planning time and thus improve their actual task performance. The next section attends to this issue.

7.5 Training task planning

A crucial issue which has not received enough attention in the task planning literature is understanding what learners do during the planning time and whether they can be trained to make use of effective planning strategies in order to promote their task performance. As Skehan (2018b) contends, planning is imagined preparation and if learners plan without the knowledge of what to plan and how to plan, their planned thoughts would be forgotten (Skehan, 2018b). In order to explore the activities that learners engage in while planning and the transferability of the knowledge of effective planning strategies to actual task performance, studies need to adopt a qualitative research methodology. As Ellis (2022) noted, researchers have expected learners to have the knowledge of planning, ignoring the possibility that some learners may have had little prior experience and may be unskilled planners. Hence, teachers need to consider the provision of training to learners to help them use their planning time efficiently. This was also strongly suggested by Kellogg (2008). Building on the assumption that learners will be better able to manage the complexity of L2 writing when they write in a way that matches their own writing strategy, Kieft *et al.* (2007) included training in how to do pre-task planning for writing argumentative texts via two types of writing instruction. In the first planning condition, learners were asked to think about the aim, audience, and content of the text, which was followed by rereading, evaluating, and revising the plans, and writing the text. In the second revising condition, learners wrote a "discovery" draft, and reread, evaluated, and revised the text using the same criteria as in the planning condition. Kieft *et al.* observed no differential impact of the planning condition or the revising condition. However, the effectiveness of the planning form of writing instruction interacted with participants' writing strategies such that the revision condition was fruitful for those with an undeveloped writing strategy, whereas the planning condition worked for those with a relatively developed writing strategy.

In another study, Gauthier (2007) investigated the effectiveness of providing training, yet her results were not encouraging since her participants who were high-school learners of L2 French were already familiar with ways of effectively planning their essays. Nevertheless, the results of this study led Gauthier to conclude that offering training might in fact profit the less-proficient writers, advising teachers to experiment with training learners to engage in appropriate pre-task planning. Khezrlou's (2020b) recent small-scale study was a response to this call which provided Iranian learners of English with Pang and Skehan's (2014) operating principles through a training program before narrative writing. The findings were promising since learners could successfully enhance their post-test task performances in terms of CAF, with accuracy reaching a comparatively smaller effect size. Furthermore, the results of retrospective interviews explicated that the participants favored the training program in facilitating the organization and expression of their thoughts based on their plans.

Although more research on training pre-task planning is needed to arrive at robust conclusions particularly about the use of training alternatives different from Pang and Skehan, whether training can endure its effectiveness through time, how long training needs to be and how many sessions are optimal, and how it works for different proficiency learners, the findings of existing studies can inform some pedagogical decisions. L2 teachers could decide on task conditions such as pre-task planning to provide space for learners to think about and channel their resources and focus on language needed for task performance. For this purpose, it is vital to equip learners with the knowledge of the right set of planning techniques to promote independent and effective task performance as well as enhanced L2 production quality in terms of CAF (Khezrlou, 2020b).

Conclusion

Task planning has attracted considerable attention in SLA and TBLT research and has become an area of inquiry in its own right (Ortega, 2005). This interest in planning lies in two principal reasons: theoretical and pedagogical. Theoretically, planning is related to the constructs of processing capacity, attention and focus on form. And, from a pedagogical perspective, it is clear that language production in L2, be it oral or written, may pose challenges on the part of L2 learners due to their limited linguistic resources. This is particularly the case when L2 learners carry out tasks that are cognitively demanding under time pressure. To enable learners to cope with this difficulty, teachers can provide them with planning time before and/or during the task. In effect, research exploring the impact of planning L2 oral production has confirmed the value of pre-task planning regarding L2 production speech quality particularly in terms of fluency and complexity, and there is some evidence to suggest that online planning benefits accuracy rather than complexity or fluency. This pattern of findings in previous studies can be explained in light of the planning behaviors learners use during the time allotted for planning. Planning without assistance may be difficult for learners particularly those at lower levels of proficiency, thereby leading them to set unrealistic and over-reaching goals to achieve during this time. The point is that research needs to move in the direction of figuring out what effective planners do and if those behaviors can be transferred to less effective planners. Consequently, both teachers and learners would be better able to manage their planning activities to attain successful L2 task performance.

8
Building on Task Performance

Introduction

Apart from task repetition, which was discussed in detail in Chapter 6, there are other post-task activities that are used to build on the main task performance. The objective of using post-task activities is to provide learning opportunities by addressing the linguistic features that had been shown to be challenging for L2 learners in the main task, and also to engage them in reflective activities (Ellis *et al.*, 2020). As overviewed in Chapter 5, some TBLT scholars suggest that a concern for attention to form needs to arise naturally in the post-task stage and therefore should only be addressed at this stage (Skehan, 1998; Willis, 1996). Long (2016) is also a proponent of a focus on forms in the post-task stage of a lesson due to its reactivity. The presumption is that the task itself makes linguistic features salient, enabling the teacher to keep track of the salient aspects when they are noticed by the learners (Schmidt, 1994). Thus, the performance of the task provides opportunities for the teacher to attract attention to the noticed features through using instructional practices to promote understanding or consolidation of the features at the post-task stage. The quintessence of post-task attention to form is that the language that is attended to is not pre-selected; rather, it emerges when the learner performs a task (Ellis *et al.*, 2020). This chapter outlines the necessity of using different techniques to provide learners with opportunities to attend to the language which was found to be difficult during task performance. These activities come in many forms, but this chapter will attend to transcriptions of one's performance of the task, task modeling, reflection on different features of task performance, and corrective feedback. I will explain the viability and effectiveness of each option in relation to research findings.

Transcription

It is now accepted that engaging learners in carrying out a post-task transcription activity following a speaking task can direct their attention to form (Hsu, 2019). This is because doing a transcription leads learners to listen to and jot down their own spoken output, compelling them to analyze their own performance (Foster & Skehan, 2013). As Cooke (2013) rightly remarked, an utterance which might have seemed accurate in the task performance could be found to be erroneous when the speech is transformed into the written text. Consequently, learners are driven to focus on the linguistic form that is used, which would attract their attention to the errors or may encourage them to dedicate more attention to linguistic choices they make during performance (Foster & Skehan, 2013), bringing about "pushed output" (Swain & Lapkin, 2001) that could lead to further development.

Empirically, a small body of studies in SLA (e.g., Cooke, 2013; Foster & Skehan, 2013; Lynch, 2001, 2007; Mennim, 2003; Stillwell et al., 2010) have investigated post-task transcribing activities. Lynch (2001), for instance, asked participants to listen to the recording of their oral task performance, select an extract of 90–120 seconds, and transcribe it. Subsequently, the learners were asked to review, revise, and edit the transcripts. Lynch found that the learners were able to notice a large number of points for change, particularly with respect to grammar and accurate expression, and their modifications were principally for the better. Stillwell et al. (2010) revealed comparable findings. In contrast, however, Foster and Skehan (2013) explored whether anticipation of the post-task transcribing activity or the post-task transcribing activity itself was what was important. They found that prediction resulted in higher narrative complexity and accuracy but the act of transcribing (without revision/edits) itself did not. Two recent studies by Hsu (2019) and Hassanzadeh-Talesh et al. (2021) looked into the joint effects of task repetition with post-task transcribing on L2 learners' task performance in terms of CAF. They both used oral narrative tasks and asked the control TR group to repeat the task with no transcription and an experimental group to engage in transcription after the main task performance. The obtained findings in the two studies, however, were different. Although Hsu found that the post-task transcribing led to more accurate speech in repeated tasks and was also carried over to a new task—albeit at the expense of fluency and complexity—Hassanzadeh-Talesh *et al.* did not reveal any benefits for post-task transcription in any of the CAF dimensions. They suggested a combination of post-task transcribing with additional pedagogical interventions to ensure L2 development.

Task modeling

Collins COBUILD English Course (Willis & Willis, 1988) was one of the early proposals to underline the potential of modeling. This course includes six methodological stages: (1) introduction that comprises some language modeling to prepare for the task, (2) task performance entailing a main focus on fluency, (3) planning a presentation of the task outcomes with a focus on accuracy, (4) reporting the results, (5) listening to/reading native speakers' performance of the task learners themselves have just performed, and (6) analysis of the language they have heard along with several chunks from the learners' corpus, on which they base their generalizations about the language. The COBUILD course intended to implement a meaning-oriented analytic approach: learners come across language in use, and they examine the language which is meaningful for them rather than decontextualized, sentence-level examples. Lynch (2018) also substantiates the contextualized and meaning-based nature of modeling, arguing that using sample performances of the same tasks by native speakers or proficient language users would encourage learners to self-correct through noticing the gap between their own performance and the models. Benefits of task modeling in promoting noticing and language learning have also been spelled out in the SLA literature (Ellis *et al.*, 2020). For example, learners are more likely to self-repair independently when they have the opportunity to compare the correct model with their own utterances. Moreover, by motivating the learners to simply notice their errors rather than doing so during language production, beginning level learners who may not be proficient enough for productive language use may experience less embarrassment.

Based on the above arguments on the role of task modeling in enhancing noticing, the main focus of studies in this realm naturally has been on the potential of modeling to promote noticing (Schmidt, 1990). The noticing has been operationalized as (a) the features that learners report when they write an initial draft (referred to in the literature as problematic features noticed), and (b) the features they report when they compare their draft to the model texts (referred to as features noticed). These two noticing types have mostly been determined by asking learners to write them down through note taking, or in studies using pair work, they were also coded via the recordings of learners' oral interactions (Cánovas Guirao *et al.*, 2015; Luquin & García Mayo, 2020, 2021; Yang & Zhang, 2010). The identification of the noticing types enabled the researchers to examine whether noticing could be incorporated into the final drafts, taking into account the quantity and type of incorporations and, in some cases, also illuminating whether these incorporations were related to the noticing types (Coyle & Roca de Larios, 2014; Hanaoka, 2007; Hanaoka & Izumi, 2012). The results of these studies have indicated that when learners had the opportunity to compare their writings to model texts, they mostly noticed lexical features and were able to include these aspects in their future writings. Hanaoka (2007), in particular, underscored the significant capacity of a good model in facilitating learners' identification of the linguistic aspects they need, which, in turn, enhances their opportunities to use and learn these features. In a different type of modeling, Kim and McDonough (2011) and Kim (2013) used video clips in which the researcher and the learners' English teacher modeled each task. Kim and McDonough (2011) found that watching task modeling videos promoted learners' use of a larger number of learner-initiated focus on form strategies such as translation or seeking assistance. In a similar vein, Kim (2013) reported the beneficial role of pre-task modeling in fostering learners' attention to form, particularly during the planning time, as well as their question development.

However, although research has mostly attended to reporting the noticing of features and subsequent incorporations, very few studies have attempted to investigate the overall impact of task modeling on the quality of the learners' writing. For example, Coyle and Roca de Larios (2014) compared the grammaticality of the initial and final draft of 46 Spanish learners of English (ages 11–12) working in pairs in two groups. One group was exposed to feedback through model texts and the other received direct WCF provided by the teacher. The results revealed that although the second draft in both conditions was improved in terms of incorporating a higher number of clauses, the error correction group performed better than the model text group. Nevertheless, it is well-worth noting here that these authors accepted "slight inaccuracies in spelling, lexis, grammar or concordance within the category of 'clauses'" (Coyle & Roca de Larios, 2014, p. 463), which necessitates more thorough analyses of accuracy. Khezrlou (2021d) explored whether the provision of oral and written task modeling between performances of the same oral narrative task could improve the speaking development of Iranian EFL learners in terms of CAF, both in the repeated task and a new task of the same type. Whereas the control group learners performed three tasks without receiving any intervention, the experimental groups were either exposed to oral task modeling immediately after the main task through listening to the audio recording of a native speaker narrating the same story, or they were given the typed script of the model task performance and were asked to read it. Results revealed that written task modeling was more effective than the oral task modeling in improving the subordination complexity of both the repeated and new tasks, and also enhanced the accurate verb forms in the repeated task, yet lost its effectiveness in the new task. And, although fluency in terms of articulation speed and mid-clause silent pauses was improved and sustained in the new task in all groups, only the oral task modeling led to reduction of repair in the repeated and new task performances. Hence, the results of this study indicated that to target accuracy, the written task modeling is superior in providing greater salience than the oral task modeling.

The study by Lázaro-Ibarrola (2021) aimed at exploring the potential of model texts as a WCF technique to enhance the noticing and incorporation of linguistic features in the context of collaborative writing and, consequently, to evaluate the effectiveness of model texts to help learners produce a text of better quality. The study was carried out with 33 learners of English aged 10–11 in a school context. One group performed the tasks individually and another group worked in pairs. The results spotted no significant differences between the individual and collaborative conditions and demonstrated the potential of model texts in inducing few instances of noticing while writing and also few, but more, instances of noticing while comparing with the model texts. Hence, the learners could notice and incorporate features, albeit to a lower extent than participants in previous research, which Lázaro-Ibarrola attributed to the young age and low level of participants and their lack of training. As for the types of noticing, in line with all previous studies, Lázaro-Ibarrola also reported that the lexical features attained the lion's share of noticing. These findings underline the significance of using modeling in a more guided manner and extended over multiple attempts to help learners benefit from a broader array of features. For instance, teachers could direct learners when comparing their drafts to model texts by depicting examples of the diverse categories of linguistics aspects to them.

Reflective learning practice

Reflective learning practice is a theoretically justified and learner-oriented intervention that has the potential to boost learners' focus on form during interaction. In higher education, reflective learning practice refers to a cognitive process that involves consciously thinking about and persistently analyzing one's previous experiences (Kolb, 1984; Schon, 2016). Based on the common-sense perspective, reflective learning practice simply represents thinking or a type of cognitive processing, which is done to perform a goal or attain an outcome (Moon, 2004). Nonetheless, from the academic viewpoint, reflection is generalized to encompass not only a type of thinking, but also a mental effort that takes place in a particular setting, pursues a specific structure, and is influenced by various contextual issues (Clegg, 2003). In other words, reflective practice needs to be conducted with a particular objective and deliberately structured so as to achieve specified learning outcomes. Furthermore, reflective practice shows specificities of self-regulated learning in which learners regulate and control their thinking process (Pintrich, 2000) and/or plan, monitor and evaluate their own learning (Wenden, 1987). This self-regulating attribute, which represents learner-oriented learning, has been found to significantly improve L2 learning (see Sato, 2020; Teng & Zhang, 2016).

Reflective practice is considered to guide learners towards a deep involvement with the learning process and therefore enables them to enhance subsequent performances through continuous analysis of previous performances (Kolb, 1984, 2014). Based on Kolb's (1984, 2014) four-phase model of reflective and experiential learning, reflective practice represents a learning cycle, in which learners (a) perform the activities (i.e., concrete experience), which is then followed by (b) observing and reflecting on this experience (i.e., reflective observation) to (c) develop abstract concepts and generalization (i.e., abstract conceptualization) prior to (d) testing and implementing these concepts in new settings (active experimentation), which then functions as a new concrete experience (i.e., the first stage of the cycle).

Reflective practice has been widely researched and divulged to be influential in advancing learning in different educational contexts and numerous disciplines (see Barkhuizen, 2010; Farrell, 2011). One of the functions of reflective practice in developing learning is that it alters experiential and implicit knowledge into systematic explicit knowledge, connects existing knowledge to examining the link among past experience, present performance, and future activities, and cultivates the re-arrangement of knowledge to obtain subsequent visions and accomplish both predicted and unforeseen learning outcomes (Dao *et al.*, 2021). When considered in the context of language learning, reflection on past experience in interaction is likely to raise learners' awareness through analyzing their interactional behavior and language production, which possibly motivates them to adapt their interaction behaviors and develop more attention to language form (Dao *et al.*, 2021). Although reflective learning has been extensively used and studied in language teacher training programs (Barkhuizen, 2010; Farrell, 2011), little attention has gone into exploring the role of reflective practice as a potentially effective pedagogical practice in increasing learners' attention to form. Building on the findings of two case studies, Lam (2018), highlights the significance of self-reflection in Showcase Portfolio Approach in improving learners' understanding of "where they are, where they want to go and what is next in their writing development" (p. 230). In other words, reflection on the showpiece dossiers raises learners' awareness of their writing norms and bridges the gaps between the current and preferred task performances. Self-reflection via keeping a diary is also promoted by Svalberg (2012) to appear in consciousness-raising tasks where learners appraise the task as a means to learning and engagement with language. More recently, Dao *et al.* (2021) investigated the role of self-reflection elevating 68 adolescent Vietnamese EFL learners' FonF during peer interaction. The analysis of learners' LREs indicated that reflection aided them to self-correct their linguistic errors and engage in metalinguistic conversations. The use of learned skills through practice however varied according to the learners' proficiency and perspectives about their partner's performance. Khezrlou (2021b) provided Iranian EFL learners with opportunities to self-reflect on their first task performance which was followed by two performances of the same task and a new task of the same type. The experimental group learners were asked to reflect on their main task performance by filling out a questionnaire which was developed for the study. Self-reports centered on five themes: (1) what learners think they learned during the task, (2) their evaluation of their task performance, (3) their perceptions of the design features of the task including its objective, nature, and difficulty, (4) their attitudes towards the task, and (5) their opinions about how to improve it. Self-reflection between repeated oral narrative task performances significantly improved participants' accurate use of the target structure—English regular past tense—from the main task to both the first and second repeated task performances, and, importantly, these improvements were also transferred to the new task.

In short, the results of studies conducted so far on reflected learning practice have all attested that through any type of reflective practice, learners' attention to linguistic features is increased. This is due to the mental effort that reflection requires and its concentration on a specific context and structure (Clegg, 2003). Therefore, teachers are encouraged to get learners thinking as they engage in reflection through which they can better understand their learners' capacity for change, needs, interests, and abilities, and in turn modify the instructional materials and approaches they use (Bachman & Palmer, 1996).

Corrective feedback (CF)

Another way of attracting learners' attention to form is to provide corrective feedback defined as "responses to learner utterances containing an error" (Ellis, 2006, p. 26). Since Truscott's (1996) debate on the role of WCF in L2 writing accuracy, a large amount of research has been carried out to explore its effectiveness. In her review of the theoretical background of CF, Polio (2012) posits that although some SLA theories, such as generative theory and processability theory, do not seem to advocate the role of CF, several SLA theories argue for the benefits of CF:

1) Skill acquisition theory—The explicit knowledge learned through CF can be converted into implicit and procedural knowledge, which can enhance the language learning process.
2) Cognitive interaction approaches to SLA—CF may activate multiple vital processes, such as input, output, noticing a gap, and intake, which according to SLA theory advance language acquisition.
3) Sociocultural theory (SCT)—CF facilitates language learning within the zone of proximal development, and teacher feedback, which can be considered "other-regulation," can enhance self-regulation in future task performances, all of which reflect the process of language development.

Considering all these interfaces between CF and SLA theories, the learning and teaching potential that CF presents seem to be very promising. In fact, although there was some controversy in the 1990s and early 2000s over the role of CF, there now appears to be a consensus that CF is useful.

Types of corrective feedback

Direct vs. indirect

Two major types of WCF that have attracted much attention are direct and indirect feedback. Direct feedback refers to feedback strategies that present the correct form. Indirect feedback, on the other hand, indicates the existence of an error yet does not provide the correction (i.e., by underlining the error or providing an error code). While there seems to be an agreement on the value of feedback in general, there has been a debate on what type of feedback is more influential (Nassaji, 2016). Some researchers, for example, have considered direct feedback to be more constructive than indirect feedback as it clearly shows how the error should be corrected (e.g., Bitchener, 2008; Ellis *et al.*, 2008; Khezrlou, 2023; Sheen, 2007). They have argued that the direct WCF may help learners better notice their interlanguage problems, offering them obvious information about the mismatch between the target and non-target forms (e.g., Bitchener & Knoch, 2010). Others, however, have asserted that indirect feedback is more advantageous in the long run since it engages learners in guided-learning and problem-solving activities and as a result helps them become independent learners (Ferris, 2003, 2006). Proponents of indirect feedback claim that indirect feedback is more effective in facilitating internalization of the form and more profound types of language processing (Bitchener, 2012). However, this hypothesis could not yet be confirmed since results from studies investigating the relative effectiveness of direct and indirect WCF (e.g., Chandler, 2003; Frantzen, 1995; Lalande, 1982, Robb *et al.*, 1986) are inconclusive.

Recently, Kang and Han (2015) conducted a meta-analysis using a large scope of articles on the effectiveness of WCF in learners' production of accurate language. This meta-analysis also examined direct and indirect feedback types and other factors that could influence the effects of WCF in L2 written accuracy. Kang and Han's findings demonstrated that WCF in general led to a greater level of grammatical accuracy in L2 writing; nonetheless, they also reported that the effectiveness of WCF was mediated by context, the genre of the writing task, and learner proficiency. With respect to the type of WCF, Kang and Han revealed no significant difference between indirect and direct feedback or between focused and unfocused feedback (i.e., feedback on particular linguistic features vs. feedback on all features). Nevertheless, the effect sizes of direct and focused feedback were relatively higher than those for the indirect and unfocused feedback. The findings of this meta-analysis reflect the mixed findings of previous research which compared indirect and direct WCF. In sum, the direct and indirect types can be welcomed during writing tasks. However, one might want to note that direct feedback would be more time-consuming for teachers than indirect feedback as the accurate forms also need to be provided. Yet, for indirect CF, learners might spend more time to understand how to self-repair at the expense of the amount of writing in a given time. As a result, teachers need to make appropriate decisions in accordance with the objective of their lessons.

Explicit vs. implicit

In the literature, a distinction is also made between implicit and explicit CF, which is considered relative, not absolute, since it is often challenging to categorize a single feedback type as implicit or explicit in the absence of another. Implicit feedback refers to corrections that do not provide metalinguistic information and/or are not direct about the errors in learners' productions (e.g., clarification requests and recasts), whereas explicit feedback types offer metalinguistic information (e.g., metalinguistic feedback) and/or directly corrects learners' errors (e.g., explicit correction) (see Loewen & Nabei, 2007 and Lyster & Saito, 2010, for more detailed categorizations of feedback types). A large number of studies have compared the relative effectiveness of explicit versus implicit feedback by operationalizing explicit feedback as metalinguistic feedback and implicit feedback as recasts. Generally, metalinguistic feedback is defined as the information, comments or questions concerning the accuracy of learners' utterances, and recasts are defined as target-like reformulations of learners' erroneous utterances (Lyster & Ranta, 1997). Results of previous studies provided support in favor of metalinguistic feedback (Carroll & Swain, 1993; Ellis, 2007; Ellis *et al.*, 2006; Khezrlou, 2021e; Sheen, 2007). Nevertheless, these results should be interpreted with caution, since some studies (e.g., Loewen & Nabei, 2007) have reported mixed findings and, they varied regarding methodology including task types, definition of feedback types, measures, target structure choices, and duration of treatment (see Goo & Mackey, 2013 and Lyster & Ranta, 2013, for some significant methodological issues in feedback research). Explicit feedback has also been operationalized as explicit correction. Yilmaz (2012) compared the role of explicit correction versus recasts in the development of locative and plural in Turkish. Explicit correction was provided by directly rejecting the learner's utterance ("X is wrong") followed by the explicit provision of the target-like form ("You should say Y"). Recasts reformulated the erroneous part of the learner's utterance. Yilmaz confirmed the efficacy of explicit correction compared to recasts in the oral production and comprehension tasks irrespective of time, communication mode and target structure.

    Researchers attempted to clarify the variability in the effectiveness of explicit and implicit feedback by reasoning that the better detection of corrective function particularly in the case of explicit feedback makes them effective in changing attention from meaning to form (Carroll, 2001; Lyster & Ranta, 1997). Although salience in terms of how the learner interprets feedback receives support from previous research, several other factors (i.e., psycholinguistic, social and practical) are also accountable for informing pedagogical decisions about feedback choices (Yilmaz & Granena, 2016). For example, explicit feedback types have been regarded as more interfering and likely to inhibit communication due to directly attracting learners' attention to target features, whereas more implicit CF types draw learners' attention to the features and reduce any disruption to the communication of meaning (Doughty & Williams, 1998). Explicit feedback is also more time-consuming. Long (2007) argued that "… even if more explicit alternatives are eventually found to work, or even to work better than implicit feedback of some kind, it will be at a cost to coverage of tasks, curricular subject matter, or other syllabus content" (p. 103). Furthermore, explicit feedback can be predicted to stimulate some negative emotional outcomes particularly in classroom contexts where learners' correction in front of classmates might lead to feelings of embarrassment, frustration, or anger. In support of this, Yoshida (2010) verified that teachers prevented explicit feedback not to damage learners' confidence since they considered that explicitly correcting their errors was threatening and overwhelming for the learners.

Scope of feedback: Focused vs. unfocused

Focused WCF refers to the correction of one or a few pre-selected structures, whereas unfocused WCF includes correcting all or a range of structures (Ellis *et al.*, 2008). According to Sheen (2007), focused feedback diminishes the attentional pressure on learners and therefore enhances the probability of raising awareness of a target structure, while unfocused feedback increases the attentional burden and hence declines the probability of learners' awareness of a structure or structures. To test the claims put forward by Sheen, several studies have been conducted to compare the effectiveness of focused and unfocused WCF. These mainly experimental/quasi-experimental studies have produced some major findings that have potential implications for classroom practice: (1) focused WCF is superior to unfocused WCF in developing accuracy of targeted errors (Ferris *et al.*, 2013; Rahimi, 2019; Shintani *et al.*, 2014); (2) WCF addressing one linguistic feature may be more influential than four to five linguistic structures (Ellis *et al.*, 2008; Sheen *et al.*, 2009); but then (3) the effects of several WCF strategies (direct, indirect, and metalinguistic) for focused/unfocused WCF are inconclusive (Buckingham & Aktuğ-Ekinci, 2017; Shintani *et al.*, 2014; Van Beuningen *et al.*, 2012).

As noted above, previous studies have polarized the unfocused and focused WCF in distinct designs, leading to inconclusive findings about unfocused WCF and the efficiency of focused WCF on target structures. To amplify the pedagogical benefits of WCF, Mao and Lee (2020) suggest that teachers may integrate focused and unfocused feedback in classroom practices. For instance, teachers can use both feedback types for diagnostic purposes and help learners determine their strengths and weaknesses in written accuracy, thereby empowering them to monitor their own writing accuracy development (Lee, 2017). Indeed, teachers play a substantial role in the authentic classroom context by planning for writing instruction, providing WCF and other types of feedback, and adopting pre- and post-writing instruction to reinforce the impacts of WCF (and other types of feedback) (Lee, 2020). Admittedly, Lee (2020) highlights that the decisions regarding feedback scope and types are context-dependent, such as the learners' proficiency level, the writing task, and the stage of the writing process. Focused and unfocused WCF should not be mutually exclusive; rather, based on the context and learner needs, can be provided in combination (e.g., focused WCF on the first draft and unfocused WCF on the final draft; unfocused WCF on the first or first few paragraphs and focused WCF on the remaining paragraphs) (Lee, 2020). Therefore, irrespective of the feedback scope, CF is solely a part of the whole teaching and learning process, and it is vital that the teaching practice is developed in ways to endorse feedback, for example through pre-writing/speaking grammar teaching and post-writing/speaking grammar emphasis. Additionally, CF comprises just one part of teacher feedback, and it is essential that feedback be provided on content, organization, and other aspects of learners' L2 production. Lastly, the learners also assume an important role in the writing classroom and effectiveness of CF. The usefulness of teacher CF can be promoted if learners are trained and empowered to play an active role in self- and peer correction, and if they are given opportunities to interact with peers and the teacher to achieve a deeper engagement with and processing of CF.

Timing of corrective feedback

In addition to types of CF influencing effectiveness and learning, another issue that may affect learning supported with feedback pertains to timing of feedback: immediate and delayed feedback. Although immediate feedback is presented as soon as an error occurs, delayed feedback occurs after the activity serving as the context for the correction is completed (Li *et al.*, 2016). Feedback timing figures prominently in SLA theories. For instance, the interaction hypothesis (Long, 2015) considers the optimal time to address errors—focus on form—during the negotiated interaction. The advantages for providing CF during meaning-oriented tasks include: (1) the probability of developing implicit knowledge which is employed in spontaneous L2 production, (2) its being reactive than preemptive based on the learner's developmental level, (3) putting the correct form next to the incorrect one to enable cognitive comparisons, and (4) providing a solution to learners' immediate communicative problem serving as an incentive for learning. Hence, the interaction hypothesis claims that feedback should be immediate, provided during interaction tasks, and be adjacent to errors. DeKeyser's (2007, 2015) skill acquisition theory also claims that CF "should not be delayed too much" (2007, p. 4), arguing that delayed feedback may lead to error fossilization. In contrast to these positions, there are reasons for advocating delayed feedback as well, such as the inevitability of the occurrence of errors given the evolving nature of the interlanguage system (Ellis, 2015; Ortega, 2009). Thus, with learners' progress towards higher levels of L2 proficiency, some errors would disappear due to exposure to more input and practice, and therefore feedback, if essential, needs to be delayed and only address errors that cannot be dealt with otherwise (Fu & Li, 2022).

Another justification for delayed feedback is related to its motivating nature since feedback is provided after learners struggle with the linguistic feature during the activities (Fu & Li, 2022). Lastly, delayed feedback is argued to be more straightforwardly noticed, processed, and internalized compared to the immediate feedback because learners would have more information about the linguistic feature and will thus be developmentally more prepared to benefit from feedback (Mackey & Philp, 1998).

Regardless of the importance of feedback timing in L2 learning, there has been very little attention paid to it in SLA research. Studies on delayed CF indicate that it is helpful in fostering learners' written accuracy in new texts (Bitchener & Ferris, 2012), although there is ambiguity as to whether it leads to the development of linguistic competence (Williams, 2012). Nevertheless, numerous other studies report that feedback is most useful when presented immediately (e.g., Aljaafreh & Lantolf, 1994; Arroyo & Yilmaz, 2018; Aubrey & Shintani, 2016; Fu & Li, 2022; Kang & Han, 2015; Li *et al.*, 2016). The studies that lend credence to immediate feedback have reported the gain in performance to be significantly greater with respect to means scores and effect size (Cohen's d) for learners obtaining immediate feedback than those receiving delayed feedback. For instance, Li, Ellis, and Zhu (2016) showed that the learners in the immediate feedback group accomplished higher scores in a grammaticality judgment test than those in the delayed feedback group. Immediate feedback also seems to be favored by learners compared to delayed feedback. As the results of Lefevre and Cox's (2017) study clearly indicate, when learners were presented with the choice, they wished to receive immediate than delayed feedback. Moreover, Marczak, Krajka, and Malec's study (2016) also found that the majority of participants have often referred to immediate feedback as the main benefit of e-learning assessment. Similarly, Lee's study (2013) demonstrated that learners strongly preferred explicit and immediate correction of their errors. Based on these findings, then, teachers should not feel so restricted by the pedagogic advice they obtain with respect to the timing of feedback and be prepared to experiment with immediate feedback when they consider appropriate.

Conclusion

The post-task stage in a task-based lesson includes activities that follow-up on the previous task performance (Ellis, 2003). According to Ellis (2003), the post-task phase is well-suited for attention to linguistic features in that the language focus at this stage of the task does not interfere with the actual focus on meaning any longer. The activities involve both analysis and practice activities, such as reflection on linguistic structures, transcription, task modeling, or corrective feedback that are used to make learners attend to form in the post-task stage. Studies investigating post-task strategies generally underline the importance of drawing learners' attention to form after learners have completed their task performance. There is certainly considerable scope to research the effects of different post-task FonF strategies in different instructional contexts and for different types of learners. It would be a mistake in tacitly expecting the FonF strategies to work in the same way in all instructional contexts, and this issue has been borne out by the restricted research I synthesized in this chapter. Yet, the review of studies on each of the options included in this chapter encourages teachers to consider adopting these strategies which have the potential of drawing attention to form after task completion. Teachers are suggested to make informed decisions based on their learners' needs and their instructional goals.

PART IV

ASSESSMENT

9
Task-based Language Assessment

Introduction

Task-based language assessment (TBLA) appeared as one type of alternative to traditional testing (Norris, 2016). TBLA sparked considerable attention since the early 1990s due to its clear correspondence with the development of TBLT (Skehan, 1998), and a simultaneous need for assessment that represented learners' L2 learning of target task abilities, emphasized authenticity of testing methods and rating criteria, and allowed predictions about the extent to which learners could use the language instead of solely learning rules and linguistic items (Norris *et al.*, 1998). Therefore, the validity of TBLA is judged based on the extent to which it can effectively establish a close connection between the test taker's performance during the test and their performance in the real-world. A flurry of publications appeared on the contributions of TBLA, the challenges in its design and implementation, and its value to language assessment. This chapter will sketch out a description of TBLA, its characteristics, components, the procedure for its design and implementation, the measurement of its outcomes, and suggestions for its use in the classroom particularly with the aid of technology.

Definition and characteristics of TBLA

TBLA uses tasks as main means of activating and observing language being used to gain real-life purposes and elicit interpretations of what test takers or learners can do with their language ability (Bachman, 2002; Ellis, 2003; Norris, 2016). It follows the same principles that define TBLT, yet in the testing domain. Specifically, as Shehadeh

(2012) explains, TBLA adheres to the TBLT methodology in using tasks as its core unit rather than using linguistic items. Indeed, Long and Norris (2000, p. 600) argue that "genuinely task-based language assessment takes the task itself as the fundamental unit of analysis, motivating item selection, test instrument construction and the rating of task performance." In a similar vein, the fundamental purpose and validity of TBLA, similar to TBLT, is measured against the establishment of a close connection between the test taker's performance during the test and their performance in the real-world (Shehadeh, 2012). For example, Ellis (2003) views TBLA as a way of attaining a close link between the test performance—what the test taker does during the test—, and the criterion of performance in terms of what the test taker is expected to do in the real-world. Accordingly, Ellis considers assessment tasks as "devices for eliciting and evaluating communicative performances from learners in the context of language use that is meaning-focused and directed towards some specific goal" (p. 279).

Shehadeh (2012) identifies four key characteristics of TBLA: First, it is a formative assessment since the evaluation constitutes a part of a task-based lesson aimed at fostering L2 learning and teaching, rather than assessment of learning outcomes, as is the case with summative tests. A summative test is "a test given at the end of a course of instruction that measures or 'sums up' how much a student has learned from the course" (Richards & Schmidt, 2010, p. 573). As a result, the major objective of a summative test is to evaluate learners' demonstration of their linguistic knowledge. In contrast, the main goal of TBLA "is not to measure the display of linguistic knowledge, nor to assign learners to broadly defined levels of language ability, but to ascertain whether students can use the L2 to accomplish target tasks" (Long & Norris, 2000, p. 600). Second, TBLA is a performance-referenced assessment which intends to provide information about learners' capacity to use context-bound language. In other words, TBLA evaluates a specific performance of learners in order to ensure the learners' capability to use the L2 to achieve real target tasks. Third, it is a direct assessment entailing the evaluation of language abilities such that tasks directly measure the test taker's performance as in information-transfer test tasks (e.g., information-gap, opinion-gap, and reasoning-gap tasks). Shehadeh warns that direct assessment still requires inferencing since the ability is inferred from the observed performance. Lastly, TBLA is an authentic assessment due to the fact that it involves either real-world language use or the types of language processing employed in real-world language use. Thus, due to their obvious relevance within the TBLT classes and programs and their notable benefits for language assessment, not only have task-based tests continued to exert important roles in classroom-based testing, but their use—often coupled with emerging technological affordances—has extended within this and other assessment contexts in order to accommodate the real-world needs of test users. Teachers, admissions officers, employers, and others pursue clear indications of the extent to which language learners can communicate in a target language (Norris, 2016).

Components of TBLA

Task-based language assessment consists of three basic components: a test task, an implementation procedure, and a performance measure:

Test task design and selection

There are two approaches to test task design and task selection in TBLA: the first is the construct-centered approach or the direct system-referenced tests. System-referenced tests measure knowledge of language as a system without taking any specific context or use into account (Baker, 1990). In such tests, the task is used merely to obtain samples of the test taker's linguistic competence, as in oral proficiency interviews or multiple-choice reading comprehension tests based on texts adapted for testing purposes (Robinson, 1996). As Pellegrino and Wilson (2015) stated, in the construct-centered approach, the selection and development of assessment tasks, as well as the scoring rubrics and criteria, and the modes and style of reporting are informed by the construct to be measured and the most appropriate ways of obtaining evidence about a learner's proficiency with that construct based on a language learning and language use theory. Pellegrino *et al.* (2001, p. xx) specified the following developmental steps in the process of assessment design and development in a construct-centered approach:

- Specifying the constructs to be assessed in language detailed enough to guide task design;
- Identifying the inferences that the assessment should support;
- Laying out the type of evidence needed to support those inferences;
- Designing tasks to collect that evidence, modeling how the evidence can be assembled and used to reach valid conclusions; and
- Iterating through the previous stages to refine the process, especially as new evidence becomes available.

The advantages of construct-centered tests lie in their generalizability to several different test samples and their easy development and administration. Moreover, their disadvantage relates to their artificial appearance and lack of face validity because the purpose of language teaching programs is to develop holistic procedural skills (Robinson, 1996).

The second approach to test task design and task selection is called the work-sample approach or the direct performance-referenced test. This approach includes the analysis of target situations to identify what tasks the test taker will need to transact in the real-world. This approach is employed with tasks that intend "to find out what a learner can do in a particular situation" (Ellis, 2003, p. 286). As Baker (1990) remarks, the field of language teaching began moving away from the use of strictly system-referenced tests such as test of English as a foreign language (TOEFL) and discrete-point tests of individual skills in the seventies, towards more integrative performance-referenced tests. The stimulus for this movement was the obvious incongruity between the notional-functional approaches to developing language which underscored the importance of communicative language use, and the tests available for assessing such an approach (Delamere, 1985).

The distinction between these two approaches to test task design and task selection, however, should not mean that they are mutually exclusive; rather, as suggested by several TBLT proponents (Ellis, 2003; Robinson 1996), a combination of performance- referenced and system-referenced task-based tests would be vital and useful. In this way, the perspective of TBLT about task as a means to internalize linguistic knowledge and skill which can be used outside the domain of the target tasks is met. Brown, Hudson, Hudson, and Bonk (2000) exhibited the possibility of such integration. They developed test tasks about different language topics such as food, health, work and so forth through the following steps:

- Needs analysis: several textbooks and language teaching materials were examined to select a set of tasks relevant to the learners' needs.
- Selecting and sequencing tasks: Skehan's (1996, 1998) three task difficulty components—code command, cognitive operations, and communicative adaptation—were used as a framework for categorizing possible sources of task difficulty in the test tasks.
- Rating scales: two different types of scales were developed for rating the test takers' performances: task-dependent and task-independent. Task-dependent rating scale intended to remove the researchers from the process as much as possible in order to simulate the conditions under which such scales might be developed in actual language programs. The task-independent rating scale was designed to help raters estimate each learner's general level of language performance across numerous types of tasks that in turn entailed different abilities in code command, cognitive operations, and communicative adaptation.
- Self-rating scale: immediately after completing the test tasks, participants were asked to complete self-rating sheets to elicit their perceptions about the difficulty of tasks, task performance and accomplishment, and the relationship between familiarity and task success.

Brown *et al.* concluded that the test tasks and instruments that were developed based on these steps greatly maintained fidelity with target communication tasks through the careful simulation of task characteristics and associated realia within testing conditions.

Implementation of test task

There are two procedures concerning the implementation of test tasks: The first is planning time. It is well-recognized that language test developers should develop conditions that enable test takers to produce their best possible performance: to "bias for the best"

(Swain, 1985, p. 42). Research findings in instructed SLA underline the effectiveness of pre-task planning in the process of L2 speech production (Ellis, 2005; O'Sullivan, 2012; Skehan, 2016; see Chapter 7). Therefore, there is a convincing argument for planning to be involved as part of speaking and writing tests to bias for the best and for test takers to show their full capabilities. As O'Sullivan (2012) notes, "if we add it, performance improves; remove it or reduce it, and performance worsens" (p. 235). Despite the suggested benefits to test takers, research still does not have a clear perspective of the influence on test scores of including a period of pre-task planning. Findings of previous studies in language testing are mixed, but they generally denote that planning may not considerably affect test results (Elder & Iwashita, 2005; Elder & Wigglesworth, 2006; Nitta & Nakatsuhara, 2014; Wigglesworth, 1997). This is in stark opposition to findings reported in TBLT, where pedagogically oriented research has constantly attested the impacts of pre-task planning on task performance. Nevertheless, as the results of O'Grady (2019) confirmed, the role of planning time in test task performance is largely mediated by the task type and the test taker's level of proficiency. O'Grady revealed that the low-level test takers benefitted from the extra planning time more than the higher-level participants, and the picture-based tasks had more of an influence on test scores than on the non-picture-based tasks, where the test takers were free to specify the content they discussed. These findings, then, corroborate Skehan's (2009) argument that narrating a series of images that include obligatory content poses challenges during speech formulation particularly for the low-ability learners who are, thus, in a better position to benefit from the planning time to compensate for limitations in their language knowledge to complete the tasks. In short, L2 speaking tests developed particularly for low-level test takers may hence entail a period of planning to meet Swain's (1985, p. 42) requirement that tests should "bias for the best" performance.

The second implementation procedure concerns the interlocutor in oral test tasks. The role of the addressee (familiar or unfamiliar, native speaker or nonnative speaker) significantly impacts the test taker's performance on an assessment task (Shehadeh, 2012). For example, some researchers have found that to obtain the "best performance" from the test taker, it may be optimal to have the candidates interact with another nonnative rather than a native speaker (e.g., Wigglesworth, 2001). Another pertinent factor in classroom assessment contexts is variability in language proficiency among the test takers. Previous research led to contradictory conclusions about the influence of interlocutor proficiency on test performance. Nakatsuhara (2004) investigated the discourse produced when different combinations of higher- and lower-proficiency candidates carried out a problem-solving task and revealed no differences in the aspects of interactional contingency, goal orientation, and quantitative dominance. Hence, Nakatsuhara concluded that candidates' different proficiency levels had little impact on conversation type, although in mixed pairings of higher- and lower-proficiency individuals, the higher-proficiency test taker spoke more and initiated more topics. In addition to these interlocutor aspects, Lazaraton (1996) identified eight interviewer behaviors that affected the test takers' discourse and the ratings. Although some behaviors such as topic priming (introducing a topic before asking a question) supported the candidate, others such as using statements as question prompts (which tend to elicit simplified yes/no answers); supplying vocabulary or completing turns; giving evaluative responses after a candidate's answer; echoing and/or correcting responses; repeating questions with slowed speech, more pausing and over-articulation; drawing conclusions for candidates (this may deprive candidates of opportunities to speak); and rephrasing questions tended to impede the performance. Gender of the examiner and/or candidate(s) is another factor that led to varied results. Brown and McNamara (2004) reviewed several quantitative and qualitative studies of the impact of gender in speaking assessment and concluded that the effect of gender is greatly complex and that existing studies "do not support any simple, deterministic idea that gender categories will have a direct and predictable impact on test processes and test outcomes" (p. 533).

Performance measurement

There are two main methods for the measurement of the performance elicited from the TBLA tests: direct assessment of task outcomes and external rating. The first method, as the name implies, refers to the observation of the performance of a task with the assessor either making a judgment or not. The judgment in the direct method of assessment is objective since the test taker either scores a solution correct or incorrect in performing the task (Shehadeh, 2012). An example of direct assessment of task outcomes is a closed task which leads to a performance that is either right or wrong, such as in locating a journal article about a specific topic in a library (Robinson & Ross, 1996). As Ellis (2003) highlights, this method enjoys providing an objective measurement, requiring no judgment on the part of the assessor, and is simple and quick.

External rating as the second performance measure includes external judgment and is therefore more subjective. This measure also encompasses the use of a scale in a holistic or analytic format. For instance, scales could be developed for the measurement of the overall linguistic ability versus the four language skills (Shehadeh, 2012). Examples of this assessment entail judging that the learner's speaking ability is at the "expert" level in the oral interview component of the old IELTS test which specifies that the learner "can speak with authority on a variety of topics; can initiate, expand, and develop a theme" (Ellis, 2003, p. 300). The external rating helps the assessor to identify the learner's competencies to be measured in more functional terms.

Uses of TBLA

Considering the association between tasks and language learning, it should be clear that TBLA can and should play a vital role in assessments used for classroom and educational program purposes (Norris, 2018). Although details are beyond the scope of this chapter, there exist several needs which are effectively met by TBLA regarding teaching and learning, such as: (a) achievement testing that stresses learning outcomes with respect to the ability to use the target language to achieve real-world purposes (e.g., Fischer *et al.*, 2011); (b) formative assessment that presents opportunities to raise awareness and offer feedback to learners and teachers regarding learners' language development en route to communicative competence (e.g., Byrnes, 2002; Weaver, 2013); and (c) correspondence of assessment practices with curriculum and teaching, with both advocating a common target of L2 ability for use (e.g., Byrnes *et al.*, 2010). Furthermore, as Norris (2018) underlines, particular features of language proficiency development can only be effectively measured via task-based designs, such as learners' abilities to integrate sociopragmatic and pragmalinguistic knowledge in achieving highly context-oriented target tasks (see Timpe-Laughlin, 2018). The task-based approach to assessing pragmatics is intended to ensure that assessment tasks obtain test-takers' pragmatic performances reflective of real-life contexts, enabling the measurement of a range of pragmatic abilities. For instance, Youn (2015) validated task-based pragmatic assessment materials, such as assessment tasks and task-dependent rating criteria, in an English for academic purposes (EAP) setting according to a needs analysis of pragmatic learning perceived by stakeholders (Youn 2018).

Undeniably, designing TBLA that can successfully meet a range of planned uses and outcomes is not without its challenges. One principal issue in implementing TBLA within classrooms and programs is related to the collection of extended task performances from all learners, rating or scoring those performances according to meaningful criteria, and presenting feedback to guide learning (Norris, 2018). These challenges, nevertheless, can be reduced thanks to technological developments and affordances. For instance, complicated interactive scenarios may be developed and conveyed by means of a computer. In this way, as Norris (2018) maintains, learners would be (a) virtually embedded within a simulated environment that requires language use to complete authentic tasks; (b) provided with different types of authentic input to create a communicative context; (c) connected with interlocutors, to present audiences for communication; (d) supported in their performances with scaffolds (e.g., guiding questions, replay of audio/video); and (e) recorded as they complete tasks (e.g., video, audio, writing, on-screen behaviors; see an example in Wolf *et al.*, 2017). Norris (2018, p. 15) clarifies that:

> Providing such technology-mediated task-based assessments may alleviate a heavy burden from teachers, who otherwise would typically assume responsibility for all of these steps; teachers, then, can turn their attention to observing performances, grading, providing feedback, and pursuing related learning-oriented activities.

Furthermore, there are specific dimensions of task-based language performance which are gradually becoming more responsive to automated scoring and feedback by the computer. Developments in natural language processing, machine learning, speech recognition, and writing evaluation already facilitate the use of automated scoring of writing and speaking tasks for particular measurement purposes (e.g., Yannakoudakis *et al.*, 2018; Zhu *et al.*, 2020), and automated formative feedback in relation to linguistic dimensions of task performances is undoubtedly practicable (e.g., Hegelheimer & Heift, 2017).

Moving forward

As Carless (2012) clearly asserted, the use of teacher assessment in traditional examination-based systems is a strong obligation to make changes in the assessment practice and a challenge to teachers' workloads and mindsets. The challenge lies in traditional examination-oriented systems in which the test that focuses on grammar, vocabulary, and reading comprehension can hinder the implementation of TBLA (Ng & Tang, 1997). Language tests in these systems constitute a main component in success in the pursuit of individual well-being and forthcoming employment opportunities. For example, Cheng (2008) states that the high rank of English tests in China does not assist teaching yet drives it. Carless (2012) emphasizes that in such settings, there is a possibility that candidates sometimes with the help of the tutors may aim at disrupting the objectives of the test developers. He provides an example from Luk (2010) which reported that the analysis of test interaction reflected the candidates' plotting to produce utterances that helped them seem to be effective interlocutors in order to gain scores rather than for authentic communication (Carless, 2012).

The use of teacher assessment in examination-based systems, at the same time, can lead the teachers to alter their mindsets stemming from the uselessness of such systems. They will then be able to shift their attention to TBLA which is a more impressive assessment tool. For this reason, over the past two decades, the high-stakes examinations have put their emphasis more on oral performance and the examinations have become increasingly task-based (Carless, 2012). Of course, a great deal more research is needed in TBLA. For instance, there are still open questions about the extent to which a formative assessment cycle supports the development of long-term learning capacities (Carless, 2012). Black and Wiliam (2003) point out that an assessment can only be expected to fulfill formative purposes if it promotes learners' learning. Perhaps, the adoption of formative assessment in relation to TBLA would be more utilized if there were opportunities for engagement with the growing educational literature on formative assessment (e.g., Schildkamp *et al.*, 2020) and developments in dynamic assessment (e.g., Poehner, 2018).

With respect to the implementation of formative assessment in TBLT, it is recognized that assessment practice in a classroom acts formatively to the extent that it stresses the centrality of learning by learners (Gan & Leung, 2020). Therefore, notions of TBLT and formative assessment naturally join in interesting ways. Wiliam (2011) notes two aspects that are specifically vital in designing classroom assessment that promotes student learning. One is that there should be not only recognition of the gap between learners' existing and intended performance but also evidence that plainly indicates the types of pedagogical activities likely to bring about improving performance in learners. The second requirement is that the learners engage in activities to enhance learning. Wiliam further recommends five 'key strategies' to ensure that the two aspects are implemented: (1) elucidating learning intentions and success criteria; (2) engineering useful questioning and classroom discussions; (3) providing feedback that moves learners forward; (4) encouraging learners to be owners of learning; and (5) motivating learners to act as learning resources for one another. As such, the promise of formative assessment as a facilitator of student learning in everyday L2 classes can be accomplished. Nonetheless, it is worth highlighting that teachers' lack of clear conceptions about TBLT and learning inevitably impeded the implementation of formative assessment. This suggests that effective TBLT teacher training is a prerequisite for success of formative assessment in L2 classrooms (Gan & Leung, 2020).

Pedagogically, then, teachers need to be trained about the principles underlying TBLA. Shehadeh (2012) rightly attributes the popularity of traditional, examination-oriented systems in various parts of the world to the teachers' lack of knowledge about TBLA, its effectiveness, and appropriate use in their classes. He also notes that many teachers, particularly in EFL/English as a second language (ESL) contexts, consider tasks as another type of the traditional exercises. Finally, a lot of teachers hold alienating views towards TBLA which make it unfeasible in their specific teaching contexts or educational settings. Evidently, more studies are needed to remove these obstacles in the development, implementation, application, and utilization of TBLA. Brindley (1994) has long ago contended that the challenge for researchers and test developers in TBLA is to create a method that offers valid and reliable measurements in assessments that are "complex, qualitative, and multidimensional, rather than uniform and standardized" (p. 90). This challenge is still the case today, making it worthwhile to work on this objective in order to tap into the test taker's ability with as much precision as possible, which is a fundamental feature of TBLA.

Conclusion

Clearly, tasks seem to play an increasingly prominent role in different levels of and uses for language assessment. In fact, accumulating examples from different settings around the world (e.g., Adair-Hauck *et al.*, 2006; Davison, 2007; East, 2015; Van Gorp & Deygers, 2013) have begun to show evidence that TBLA innovations can exert a remarkable positive impact on language teachers, learners, and educational systems, as they are gradually and carefully put into practice. Of course, more research still needs to be done into TBLA, but it is already apparent that task research is relevant to the design of assessment procedures and to the interpretation of results. There is also the crucial argument that a task-oriented approach to assessment may prove fruitful in reconciling the interactive-ability and real-life approaches by demonstrating how tasks can be based on researched characteristics and conditions, and by examining the processing demands required for task completion. Accordingly, a more appropriate foundation for making test-linked generalizations can be made. In sum, task-based tests, although difficult to design and administer, are a logical consequence of task-based syllabuses.

PART V

CONCLUSION

10
Conclusion

Introduction

The aim of this chapter is to draw together the conclusions reached in the previous chapters, and to offer an overall assessment of TBLT. This chapter intends to identify and include related commentary on some important themes which are still in need of attention and exploration that have arisen throughout the book. We will briefly look at what was covered and also at what might come next.

Task design and task implementation

Skehan (1996) has underscored the importance of differentiating between task design and task implementation variables. In this book, issues related to both task design and task implementation conditions were taken into consideration. The selection of task in the syllabus is significant as it will affect the performance of learners. As explained in Chapter 2, the real-world relationship needs to be taken into account in the selection of a particular task, and learners should make use of their linguistic resources to complete it. Nevertheless, needs analysis is not the sole prerequisite for the selection of tasks, and teaching issues, prior experience and learner interests are also important factors to involve in task design. Therefore, the main point in task selection is the suitability of a task in a task-based syllabus and its potential to achieve appropriate pedagogic purposes. The more difficult challenge, however, lies in justifying not just task selection but also task sequencing. There are a number of generalizations about particular task characteristics that can be used to sequence tasks, as outlined in Chapter 4. Unfortunately, however, the identification of the complexity of a task as workplan and its sequencing based on the existing proposals still remain unclear. As

Skehan (2016, pp. 44–45) contends, "some insights have been achieved about task qualities that have systematic connections with performance, but not much more than that—certainly not enough to be the basis for practical intervention beyond identifying useful individual tasks". In contrast, the prominence of task implementation conditions has been attested to fairly consistently in previous research which can also be used as criteria to adjust the complexity of task performance, for example, through providing or withholding planning time, visual support and so forth. Condition-oriented research, then, is more amenable for translation into pedagogy and methodological decision making than task design choices, enabling teachers to address areas of performance in need of improvement in a way that balances form and meaning (Skehan, 2016). This will truly work with any selected task type and for whatever instructional aim. Along these lines, implementation conditions that enhance any or all performance dimensions (i.e., CAF) could be determined, as well as the combined impact of design and implementation variables (e.g., pre-task planning and task structure). Then, this information could be used by teachers intending to attain specific instructional purposes, considering the current position of their learners.

In support of the feasibility and clarity of identifying and applying effective task conditions to classroom practices, Skehan (2016) also notes the simplicity of using different task conditions in instructional settings. For example, task repetition is a relatively easy and uncomplicated technique to employ in the classroom, with perhaps the only difficulty being decisions on the details of repetition, such as the number of repetitions, interval of repetition and similar issues that could be identified based on particular learners' characteristics, level of proficiency, and needs. In a similar vein, task planning, explicit instruction, and post-task conditions would similarly be straightforward to utilize and can be used with several different types of tasks. Moreover, "to the extent that research findings of performance improvements are replicated in the pedagogic situations, then learners' motivation levels may be enhanced if they realize higher performance levels have been achieved" (Skehan, 2016, p. 45). Skehan also notes that teachers have a particularly important role to play here, which is, nevertheless, not explored so far. Providing learners with opportunities to perform tasks under particular conditions over a relatively long time frame might shed important light on how task conditions could be trained to reinforce their effectiveness as learners get used to their application. For example, as explicated in Chapter 7, training learners to use effective pre-task planning strategies is a newly emerging area of research with a high potential for arriving at more durable and robust effects on learners' task performance. To achieve this purpose, it is vital to explore the cognitive and affective processes entailed in the different types of implementation options, which, unfortunately, has not received much attention in the field.

Contextual adaptations to TBLT

The necessity of adopting teaching approaches which are situated in local needs and values has been well-established over the last couple of decades. Based on this line of thinking, a vital issue lies in understanding how TBLT might be adapted to meet the goals of instruction in EFL contexts, or vice versa, and the extent to which instructional conventions may need to change in order for effective language learning to occur. A possible consequence is that adaptations of TBLT may consist of some type of reconciling the global with localized methodologies (Littlewood, 2011). The opinion lying beneath such a viewpoint is the need for inclusive non-dogmatic approaches to TBLT (Carless, 2012). Within such an approach, it would be helpful to specify major aspects central to all types of TBLT and investigate further those aspects amenable to contextual adaptation.

A pertinent topic which arises in the adoption of TBLT in EFL contexts is how TBLT can be adjusted to align it with the exigencies of the existing instructional and cultural conditions. For instance, the acquisition of L2 grammatical forms is perceived differently in TBLT compared to more explicit teacher-fronted classroom settings. This issue requires contextual adaptations with regard to ways in which teaching grammar is recognized and how it is generally approached in a specific setting. This may involve some departure from traditional PPP path, criticized for restricting the learner's experience of language by focusing on a single grammatical item (e.g., Willis, 1996), if not always appreciated by classroom teachers. Nonetheless, there are still possibilities for developing productive types of PPP through the adoption of task-supported language teaching (Ellis, 2003, 2019a). This may comprise further examination of the harmonizing functions of analytic and experiential strategies, as underscored by Littlewood (2011).

Can then a modular approach be a more realistic option in some instructional contexts? To move TBLT forward, Ellis proposed a hybrid syllabus bringing TBLT and explicit instruction together. In the modular approach, no integration between meaning and form is prearranged in the syllabus. The syllabus involves two separate components: a task-based component and a structural component. The modular curriculum is in the initial stage and the structured approach is delayed until learners have developed a basic ability to communicate (Ellis, 2003). In this way, TBLT does not replace traditional language teaching approaches; rather, it is used alongside them in a complete curriculum. Nevertheless, the question that emerges here is whether TSLT is conducive to the development of implicit second language knowledge. The use of a modular approach leads to learning that is unlikely to feed directly into the learners' communicative abilities. However, it reinforces learners' explicit knowledge which based on some theories (e.g., Ellis, 1994) acts as a resource for monitoring output and for inducing focus on linguistic features that learners are exposed to in task-based input and hence indirectly and after some time facilitates implicit knowledge (Ellis *et al.*, 2020). Nevertheless, in EFL contexts where learners have limited opportunities for language use in contexts other than the classroom, and with beginner-level learners, the only access to communicative input is the classroom, and therefore tasks are needed. As such, more studies are called for to investigate the use of task-supported teaching in challenging contexts as a preparation for TBLT with the end goal of fostering communicative ability in learners.

Assessment and TBLT

A full-fledged TBLT curriculum needs to accommodate the assessment of learners' learning processes and outcomes. This component is achieved through including tests that are task-based and would encourage teachers to be innovative with assessment, which is essential for the success of all language learning programs (Norris, 2006). Well thought-out assessment practices that provide a direct link between tasks used for learning and tasks used for evaluation of learning are necessary. As noted in Chapter 9, whereas some researchers have argued that the assessment should adhere to the TBLT course goals and advocated performance-referenced assessment—that is, assessing learners on how well they enact the target tasks—(Mislevy et al., 2002; Norris, 2002; Robinson & Ross, 1996), others argue for the inclusion of construct-based assessment (Bachman, 2002). Although Bachman (2002) has defined constructs as linguistic competences, Mislevy (2010) considered the definition of a construct as linguistic competence misleading, asserting that a construct can solely be the ability to complete a task in a particular context. These arguments continue and therefore would benefit from further research.

Despite the existence of multiple definitions of TBLA, there is a dearth of studies that examine the assessments used within a particular TBLT course. The implementation of such practices necessitates the teacher to help learners understand and appropriately contextualize their task-based learning by offering opportunities in class for reflection on task outcomes, learning purposes, and standards (Winke, 2014). This can be achieved if teachers integrate formative assessment into their TBLT-oriented classes to stimulate scaffolded self-reflection, as outlined by Black (2009). Winke (2014), following a pre-task, main-task, post-task cycle in a CALL-based course, asked learners to self-assess their performances, and, interestingly, their self-assessments were highly reflective of their actual performance and agreed with the expert ratings. Winke's results make it clear that a language-focus phase in the post-task cycle provides wonderful opportunities for using formative assessment, as language testers have suggested. The important feature of this study was that the oral assessment was not segregated from the class context; rather, it was incorporated into the design of the course and had an underlying pedagogical purpose. Winke's study also highlighted the supportive role of technology in the effectiveness of task-based assessment in three ways: (a) to amplify the amount and type of target language input the learners were exposed to during tasks; (b) to present learners with numerous modes of input (visuals, speech, and captions) in order to help them decontextualize and parse the incoming streams of speech during the tasks; and (c) to obtain high-quality, post-task language performance samples that could be analyzed and documented as task-outcome achievement.

Although some studies such as Winke's have attempted to demonstrate the feasibility and effectiveness of using task-based language assessment in the classroom, research in this area has not been so extensive. There are some other initiatives in relation to TBLA which are worth exploring. For instance, dynamic assessment which provides scaffolding as an integral part of the assessment is essentially formative in nature. In dynamic assessment, the teacher and the learners engage in a dialogue to understand the learner's current level of performance on any task and exchange possible ways of improving performance for subsequent tasks. In addition, learners' roles as task directors, feedback providers, and language monitors, both of their peers' language and of their own language has not received attention in the TBLA research. As a next step, then, it may be important to carry out more longitudinal and in-depth, qualitative research over extended periods of time. TBLA opportunities are best provided in an environment that is participatory, proactive, and democratic. It is hoped that adopting tasks based on learners' needs, engaging them in self- and peer-assessment, and providing scaffolding on task performance as part of an extended, in-class, assessment process would facilitate a move towards a fully-fledged TBLT.

Concluding thoughts

The history of language teaching is replete with approaches that fall in and out of fashion. This book has shown that task-based language teaching has stood the test of time for over three decades and has grown in popularity, to include all aspects from theory building to task features to large-scale implementations. A copious amount of work has been conducted, and even more crucially, research methods have matured as a result of deeper insights gained from issues such as task design and performance measurement. The maturity of the field presents a humbling reminder that we need to adopt an objective look at where the field will go, and what contributions remain to be made in order to most effectively utilize the existing knowledge in this area. This book has provided some hints as to what directions we might take and has intended to help guide the direction of future research in the field. Of those emerging themes that seem to hold promise for further discussion and research, the training of teachers to their full potential to better understand and implement this teaching approach, the adaptation of TBLT to challenging teaching contexts, the effective incorporation of task-based assessment into the classroom context, as well as opportunities for the productive implementation of tasks and the trainability of such conditions in the class will surely continue to draw on the expertise of TBLT experts to help move the field forward. Obviously, there is a real opportunity for those interested in TBLT including practitioners, teacher trainers, material/test developers, and researchers to begin shaping the next ten years, and the next century of second language pedagogy right now.

References

Abdi Tabari, M. (2021). Task preparedness and L2 written production: Investigating effects of planning modes on L2 learners' focus of attention and output. *Journal of Second Language Writing, 52.* Advance online publication. https://doi.org/10.1016/j.jslw.2021.100814

Adair-Hauck, B., Glisan, E., Koda, K., Swender, E., & Sandrock, P. (2006). The Integrated Performance Assessment (IPA): Connecting assessment to instruction and learning. *Foreign Language Annals, 39*, 359–382.

Adams, R., & Newton, J. (2009). TBLT in Asia: constraints and opportunities. *Asian Journal of English Language Teaching, 19*, 1–27.

Ahmadian, M. J. (2011). The effect of 'massed' task repetitions on complexity, accuracy and fluency: does it transfer to a new task? *The Language Learning Journal, 39*(3), 269–280.

Ahmadian, M., & Tavakoli, M. (2011). The effects of simultaneous use of careful on-line planning and task repetition on accuracy, complexity, and fluency in EFL learners' oral production. *Language Teaching Research, 15*(1), 35–59.

Altschuld, J. W., & Witkin, B. R. (2000). *From needs assessment to action: Transforming needs into solution strategies.* Sage.

Amelohina, V., Nicolás-Conesa, F., & Manchón, R. M. (2020). Effects of task repetition with the aid of direct and indirect written corrective feedback: A longitudinal study in an out-of-school context. In R. M. Manchón (Ed.), *Writing and language learning: Advancing research agendas* (pp. 145–181). John Benjamins.

Amiryousefi, M. (2016). The differential effects of two types of task repetition on the complexity, accuracy, and fluency in computer-mediated L2 written production: A focus on computer anxiety. *Computer Assisted Language Learning, 29*(5), 1052–1068.

References

Anderson, J. R. (1993). *Rules of the mind*. Lawrence Erlbaum Associates.

Aubrey, S., Lambert, K., & Leeming, P. (2020). The impact of first as opposed to second language pre-task planning on the content of problem-solving task performance. *Language Teaching Research*. Advance online publication. https://doi.org/10.1177/1362168820917844

Aubrey, S., & Philpott, A. (2022). Use of the L1 and L2 in strategic planning and rehearsal for task performances in an online classroom. *Language Teaching Research*. Advance online publication. https://doi.org/10.1177/13621688221077421

Azkarai, A., & García Mayo, M. D. P. (2016). Task repetition effects on L1 use in EFL child task-based interaction. *Language Teaching Research, 21*(4), 480–495.

Bachman, L. F. (2002). Some reflections on task-based language performance assessment. *Language Testing, 19*, 453–76.

Bachman, L. F., & Palmer, A. S. (1996). *Language testing in practice: Designing and developing useful language tests*. Oxford University Press.

Baker, D. (1990). *A guide to language testing*. Edward Arnold.

Baralt, M., Gilabert, R., & Robinson, P. (2014). *Task sequencing and instructed second language learning*. Bloomsbury.

Barkhuizen, G. (2010). An extended positioning analysis of a pre-service teacher's better life small story. *Applied Linguistics, 31*, 282–300.

Basterrechea, M., & Leeser, M. J. (2019). Language-related episodes and learner proficiency during collaborative dialogue in CLIL. *Language Awareness, 28*(2), 97–113.

Basturkmen, H., Loewen, S., & Ellis, R. (2004). Teachers' stated beliefs about incidental focus on form and their classroom practices. *Applied Linguistics, 25*(2), 243–272.

Benati, A. (2020). The effects of structured input and traditional instruction on the acquisition of the English causative passive forms: An eye-tracking study measuring accuracy in responses and processing patterns. *Language Teaching Research*. Advance online publication. https://doi.org/10.1177/1362168820928577

Bird, S. (2010). Effects of distributed practice on the acquisition of second language English syntax. *Applied Psycholinguistics, 31*, 635–650.

Bitchener, J. (2008). Evidence in support of written corrective feedback. *Journal of Second Language Writing, 17,* 102–118.

Bitchener, J. (2012). A reflection on 'the language learning potential' of written CF. *Journal of Second Language Writing, 21,* 348–363.

Bitchener, J., & Knoch, U. (2010). Raising the linguistic accuracy level of advanced L2 writers with written corrective feedback. *Journal of Second Language Writing, 19*(4), 207–217.

Black, P. (2009). Formative assessment issues across the curriculum: The theory and the practice. *TESOL Quarterly, 43,* 519–524.

Black, P., & Wiliam, D. (2003). In praise of educational research: Formative assessment. *British Educational Research Journal, 29*(5), 623–637.

Boston, J. (2010). Pre-task syntactic priming and focused task design. *ELT Journal, 64,* 165–174.

Branden, K. (2006). *Task-based language education: From theory to practice.* Cambridge University Press.

Breen, M. (1987). Learner contributions to task design. In C. Candlin & D. Murphy (Eds.), *Language learning tasks* (pp. 23–46). Prentice Hall.

Brindley, G. (1994). Task-centered assessment in language learning programs: The promise and the challenge. In N. Bird, P. Falvey, A. Tsui, D. Allison, & A. McNeill (Eds.), *Language and learning* (pp. 73–94). Institute of Language in Education.

Brown, A., & McNamara, T. (2004). 'The devil is in the detail': Researching gender issues in language assessment. *TESOL Quarterly, 38,* 524–538.

Brown, H. D. (2007). *Teaching by principles: An interactive approach to language pedagogy* (3rd ed.). Pearson Education.

Brown, J. D. (2009). Foreign and second language needs analysis. In M. Long & C. Doughty (Eds.), *The handbook of language teaching* (pp. 269–293). Wiley-Blackwell.

Brown, J. D., Hudson, T., Norris, J. M., & Bonk, W. (2000). Performance assessment of ESL and EFL students. *University of Hawai'i working Papers in ESL, 18*(2), 99–139.

Bryfonski, L., & McKay, T. H. (2019). TBLT implementation and evaluation: A meta-analysis. *Language Teaching Research, 23*(5), 603–632.

Buckingham, L., & Aktuğ-Ekinci, D. (2017). Interpreting coded feedback on writing: Turkish EFL students' approaches to revision. *Journal of English for Academic Purposes, 26*, 1–16.

Bui, G. (2021). Influence of learners' prior knowledge, L2 proficiency and pre-task planning on L2 lexical complexity. *International Review of Applied Linguistics in Language Teaching, 59*(4), 543–567.

Bui, G., Ahmadian, M. J., & Hunter, A. (2019). Spacing effects on repeated L2 task performance. *System, 81*, 1–13.

Bui, G., & Teng, M. (2018). Exploring learners' self-reported behavioral patterns in two task-readiness conditions: A qualitative study. *Chinese Journal of Applied Linguistics, 41*, 129–149.

Butler Y. G. (2017) Communicative and task-based language teaching in the Asia-Pacific region. In N. Van Deusen-Scholl & S. May (Eds.), *Second and foreign language education: Encyclopedia of language and education* (pp. 327–338). Springer.

Butterworth, B. (1980). Some constraints on models of language production. In B. Butterworth (Ed.), *Language production* (pp. 423–459). Academic Press.

Bygate, M. (1996). Effects of task repetition: Appraising the developing language of learners. In J. Willis & D. Willis (Eds.), *Challenge and change in language teaching* (pp. 136–146). Heinemann.

Bygate, M. (1999). Task as the context for the framing, re-framing and unframing of language. *System, 27*, 33–48.

Bygate, M. (2001). Effects of task repetition on the structure and control of oral language. In M. Bygate, P. Skehan & M. Swain (Eds.), *Researching pedagogic tasks, second language learning, teaching and testing* (pp. 23–48). Longman.

Bygate, M. (2016). Sources, developments and directions of task-based language teaching. *The Language Learning Journal, 44*(4), 381–400.

Bygate, M. (2018). Introduction. In M. Bygate (Ed.), *Learning language through task repetition* (pp. 1–25). John Benjamins.

Bygate, M., & Samuda, V. (2005). Integrative planning through the use of task-repetition. In R. Ellis (Ed.), *Planning and task performance in a second language* (pp. 37–74). John Benjamins.

Byrnes, H., Maxim, H., & Norris, J. M. (2010). *Realizing advanced FL writing development in collegiate education: Curricular design, pedagogy, assessment.* In The Modern Language Journal, Monograph. Wiley-Blackwell.

Cameron, D. (2001). *Working with spoken discourse.* Sage.

Candlin, C. (1987). Towards task-based language learning. In C. N. Candlin & D. Murphy (Eds.), *Language learning tasks* (pp. 5–22). Prentice Hall.

Cánovas Guirao, J., Roca de Larios, J., & Coyle, Y. (2015). The use of models as a written feedback technique with young EFL learners. *System 52*(1), 63–77.

Carless, D. R. (2003). Factors in the implementation of task-based teaching in primary schools. *System, 31*(4), 485–500.

Carless, D. R. (2012). TBLT in EFL settings: Looking back and moving forward. In A. Shehadeh & C. A. Coombe (Eds.), *Task-based language teaching in foreign language contexts: Research and implementation* (pp. 345–358). John Benjamins.

Carpenter, S. K. (2017). Spacing effects on learning and memory. In J. T. Wixted & J. H. Byrne (Eds.), *Cognitive psychology of memory: Learning and memory: A comprehensive reference* (pp. 465–485). Academic Press.

Carroll, J. B. (1993). *Human cognitive abilities: A survey of factor-analytic studies.* Cambridge University Press.

Carroll, S. (2001). *Input and evidence: The raw material of second language acquisition.* John Benjamins.

Carroll, S., & Swain, M. (1993). Explicit and implicit negative feedback: An empirical study of the learning of linguistic generalizations. *Studies in Second Language Acquisition, 15,* 357–386.

Carver, J., & Kim, Y. (2020). French learners' past-tense development through collaborative writing tasks: The role of procedural and content repetition. *Canadian Modern Language Review, 76*(2), 114–138.

Cepeda, N. J., Pashler, H., Vul, E., Wixted, J. T., & Rohrer, D. (2006). Distributed practice in verbal recall tasks: A review and quantitative synthesis. *Psychological Bulletin, 132,* 354–380.

Chandler, J. (2003). The efficacy of various kinds of error feedback for improvement in the accuracy and fluency of L2 student writing. *Journal of Second Language Writing, 12*(3), 267–296.

Chen, J. (2020). The effects of pre-task planning on EFL learners' oral performance in a 3D multi-user virtual environment. *ReCALL, 32*(3), 232–249.

Cheng, L. (2008). The key to success: English language testing in China. *Language Testing, 25*(1), 15–37.

Clegg, K. (2003). *Improving learning through reflection*. Higher Education Academy.

Cooke, S. D. (2013). Examining transcription, autonomy and reflective practice in language development. *RELC Journal, 44*(1), 75–85.

Coughlin, P., & Duff, P. A. (1994). Same task, different activities: Analysis of SLA task from an Activity Theory perspective. In J. Lantolf and G. Appel (Eds.), *Vygotskian perspectives on second language research* (pp. 173–193). Ablex.

Coyle, Y., & Roca de Larios, J. (2014). Exploring the role played by error correction and models on children's reported noticing and output production in a L2 writing task. *Studies in Second Language Acquisition, 36*(3), 451–485.

Crookes, G. (1989). Planning and interlanguage variation. *Studies in Second Language Acquisition, 55*, 367–383.

Dao, P. (2019). Effects of task goal orientation on learner engagement in task performance. *International Review of Applied Linguistics in Language Teaching, 59*(3), 315–334.

Dao, P., Nguyen, M. X. N. C., & Chi, D. N. (2021). Reflective learning practice for promoting adolescent EFL learners' attention to form. *Innovation in Language Learning and Teaching, 15*(3), 247–262.

Davison, C. (2007). Views from the chalkface: English language school-based assessment in Hong Kong. *Language Assessment Quarterly, 4*(1), 37–68.

De Jong, N (2012). Does time pressure help or hinder oral fluency? In N. De Jong, K. Juffermans, M. Keijzer, & L. Rasier (Eds.), *Papers of the Anéla 2012 applied linguistics conference*. Eburon.

De Jong, N., & Perfetti, C. A. (2011). Fluency training in the ESL classroom: An experimental study of fluency development and proceduralization. *Language Learning, 61*(2), 533–568.

DeKeyser, R. M. (1998). Beyond focus on form: Cognitive perspectives on learning and practicing second language grammar. In C. Doughty & J. Williams (Eds.), *Focus on form in classroom second language acquisition* (pp. 42–63). Cambridge University Press.

DeKeyser, R. M. (2003). Implicit and explicit learning. In C. J. Doughty & H. M. Long (Eds.), *The handbook of second language acquisition* (pp. 312–348). Blackwell.

DeKeyser, R. M. (2010). Practice for second language learning: Don't throw out the baby with the bathwater. *International Journal of English Studies, 10*(1), 155–165.

DeKeyser, R. M. (2015). Skill acquisition theory. In B. VanPatten & J. Williams (Eds.), *Theories in second language acquisition: An introduction* (pp. 94–112). Routledge.

De la Fuente, M. J. (2006). Classroom L2 vocabulary acquisition: Investigating the role of pedagogical tasks and form-focused instruction. *Language Teaching Research, 10*, 263–295.

Delamere, T. (1985). Notional functional syllabi and criterion referenced tests: The missing link. *System, 13*, 43–47.

Doughty, C. (2001). Cognitive underpinnings of focus on form. In P. Robinson (Ed.), *Cognition and second language instruction* (pp. 204–255). Cambridge University Press.

Doughty, C., & Pica, T. (1986). 'Information Gap' tasks: do they facilitate second language acquisition? *TESOL Quarterly, 20*(2), 305–325.

Doughty, C., & Varela, E. (1998). Communicative focus on form. In C. Doughty & J. Williams (Eds.), *Focus on form in classroom second language acquisition* (pp. 114–138). Cambridge University Press.

Doughty, C., & Williams, J. (1998). *Focus on form in classroom second language acquisition*. Cambridge University Press.

Duff, P. A. (1986). Another look at interlanguage talk: Taking task to task. In R. R. Day (Ed.), *Talking to learn: Conversation in second language acquisition* (pp. 147–181). Newbury House.

Duong, P. T., Perez, M. M., Desmet, P., & Peters, E. (2021). Learning vocabulary in spoken input- and output-based tasks. *TASK, 1*(1), 100–126.

East, M. (2015). Coming to terms with innovative high-stakes assessment practice: Teachers' viewpoints on assessment reform. *Language Testing, 32*(1), 101–120.

Edwards, J. (2008). The transcription of discourse. In D. Schiffrin, D. Tannen & H. Hamilton (Eds.), *The handbook of discourse analysis* (pp. 321–348). Routledge.

Elder, C., & Iwashita, N. (2005). Planning for test performance: Does it make a difference? In R. Ellis (Ed.), *Planning and task performance in a second language* (pp. 219–239). John Benjamins.

Elder, C., & Wigglesworth, G. (2006). *An investigation of the effectiveness and validity of planning time in part 2 of the IELTS speaking test. IELTS Research Reports* (Vol. 6, pp. 1–28). IELTS Australia and British Council.

Ellis, R. (1987). Interlanguage variability in narrative discourse: Style shifting in the past tense. *Studies in Second Language Acquisition, 9*, 1–19.

Ellis, R. (1993). Second language acquisition and the structural syllabus. *TESOL Quarterly, 27*, 91–113.

Ellis, R. (1994). A theory of instructed second language acquisition. In N. Ellis (Ed.), *Implicit and explicit learning of languages* (pp. 79–114). Academic Press.

Ellis, R. (2003). *Task-based language learning and teaching*. Oxford University Press.

Ellis, R. (2005). Planning and task-based performance. In R. Ellis (Ed.), *Planning and task performance in a second language* (pp. 3–34). John Benjamins.

Ellis, R. (2006). Researching the effects of form-focused instruction on L2 acquisition. *AILA Review, 19*, 18–41.

Ellis, R. (2007). The differential effects of corrective feedback on two grammatical structures. In A. Mackey (Ed.), *Conversational interaction in second language acquisition* (pp. 339–360). Oxford University Press

Ellis, R. (2009a). Task-based language teaching: Sorting out the misunderstandings. *International Journal of Applied Linguistics, 19*(3), 221–246.

Ellis, R. (2009b). The differential effects of three types of task planning on the fluency, complexity, and accuracy in L2 oral production. *Applied Linguistics, 30*(4), 474–509.

Ellis, R. (2013). Task-based language teaching: Responding to the critics. *University of Sydney Papers in TESOL, 8*, 1–27.

Ellis, R. (2015). *Understanding second language acquisition* (2nd ed.). Oxford University Press.
Ellis, R. (2018). *Reflections on task-based language teaching*. Multilingual Matters.
Ellis, R. (2019a). Towards a modular curriculum for using tasks. *Language Teaching Research, 23*(4), 454–475.
Ellis, R. (2019b). Task preparedness. In Z. D. Wen & M. J. Ahmadian (eds.), *Researching L2 task performance and pedagogy: In honor of Peter Skehan* (pp. 15–38). John Benjamins.
Ellis, R. (2022). Does planning before writing help? Options for pre-task planning in the teaching of writing. *ELT Journal, 76*(1), 77–87.
Ellis, R., Basturkmen, H., & Loewen, S. (2002). Doing focus-on-form. *System, 30*(4), 419–432.
Ellis, R., Loewen, S., & Erlam, R. (2006). Implicit and explicit corrective feedback and the acquisition of L2 grammar. *Studies in Second Language Acquisition, 28*, 339–368.
Ellis, R., Sheen, Y., Murakami, M., & Takashima, H. (2008). The effects of focused and unfocused written corrective feedback in an English as a foreign language context. *System, 36*, 353–371.
Ellis, R., Skehan, P., Li, S., Shintani, N., & Lambert, C. (2020). *Task-based language teaching: Theory and practice.* Cambridge University Press.
Ellis, R., & Yuan, F. (2004). The effects of planning on fluency, complexity, and accuracy in second language narrative writing. *Studies in second Language acquisition, 26*(01), 59–84.
Ellis, R., & Yuan, F. (2005). The effects of careful within-task planning on oral and written task performance. In R. Ellis (Ed.), *Planning and task performance in second language learning* (pp. 167–192). Benjamins.
Erlam, R. (2016). I'm still not sure what a task is: Teachers designing language tasks. *Language Teaching Research, 20*, 279–299.
Farrell, T. (2011). Exploring the professional role identities of experienced ESL teachers through reflective practice. *System, 39*, 54–62.
Ferris, D. R., Liu, H., Sinha, A., & Senna, M. (2013). Written corrective feedback for individual L2 writers. *Journal of Second Language Writing, 22*(3), 307–329.

Fischer, J., Chouissa, C., Dugovičová, S., & Virkkunen-Fullenwider, A. (2011). *Guidelines for task-based university language testing*. European Center for Modern Languages.

Foster, P., & Skehan, P. (1996). The influence of planning on performance in task-based learning. *Studies in Second Language Acquisition, 18*, 299–324.

Foster, P., & Skehan, P. (2013). Anticipating a post-task activity: The effects on accuracy, complexity and fluency of L2 language performance. *Canadian Modern Language Review, 69*(3), 249–273.

Frantzen, D. (1995). The effects of grammar supplementation on written accuracy in an intermediate Spanish content course. *The Modern Language Journal, 79*(3), 329–344.

Fukunaga, T. (2021). L2 writing development through two types of writing task repetition. *International Review of Applied Linguistics in Language Teaching*. Advance online publication. https://doi.org/10.1515/iral-2021-0144

Fukuta, J. (2016). Effects of task repetition on learners' attention orientation in L2 oral production. *Language Teaching Research, 20*(3), 321–340.

Gan, Z., & Leung, C. (2020). Illustrating formative assessment in task-based language teaching. *ELT Journal, 74*(1), 10–19.

García-Fuentes, C., & McDonough, K. (2016). The effect of explicit instruction and task repetition on Colombian EFL students' use of politeness strategies during disagreements. *The Language Learning Journal, 46*(4), 470–482.

Gass, S. (1997). *Input, interaction, and the second language learner*. Lawrence Erlbaum.

Gass, S., Mackey, A., Alvarez-Torres, M. J., & Fernandez-Garcia, M. (1999). The effects of task repetition on linguistic output. *Language Learning, 49*(4), 549–581.

Gatbonton, E., & Segalowitz, N. (1988). Creative automatization: Principles for promoting fluency within a communicative framework. *TESOL Quarterly, 22*(3), 473–492.

Gauthier, M. (2007). *The effects of structure pretask writing plans in L1 and L2 on high school learners' ESL writing performance*. Unpublished master's thesis, University of Toronto, Canada.

Gilabert, R. (2005). *Task complexity and L2 narrative oral production*. Unpublished Ph.D. dissertation, Universitat de Barcelona, Spain.

Gilabert, R., Baron, J., & Levkina, M. (2011). Manipulating task complexity across task types and modes. In P. Robinson (Ed.), *Second language task complexity* (pp. 105–140). John Benjamins.

Godfroid, A., Ahn, J., Choi, I., Ballard, L., Cui, Y., Johnston, S., Lee, S., Sarkar, A., & Yoon, H.J. (2018). Incidental vocabulary learning in a natural reading context. An eye-tracking study. *Bilingualism: Language and Cognition, 21*(3), 563–584.

González-Lloret, M. (2015). The need for needs analysis in technology-mediated TBLT. In M. González-Lloret & L. Ortega (Eds.), *Technology-mediated TBLT: Researching technology and tasks*. John Benjamins.

Goo, J., & Mackey, A. (2013). The case against the case against recasts. *Studies in Second Language Acquisition, 35,* 127–165.

Graves, K. (2000). *Designing language courses: A guide for teachers*. Newbury House.

Gu, Q. (2021). Impact of task preparedness on L2 oral performance and strategy use: The case of Chinese EFL learners. *TASK, 1*(2), 196–226.

Hanaoka, O. (2007). Output, noticing, and learning: An investigation into the role of spontaneous attention to form in a four-stage writing task. *Language Teaching Research, 11,* 459–479.

Hanaoka, O., & Izumi, S. (2012). Noticing and uptake: Addressing pre-articulated covert problems in L2 writing. *Journal of Second Language Writing, 21*(4), 332–347.

Harris, J., & Leeming, P. (2020). The accuracy of teacher predictions of student language use in tasks in a Japanese university. In C. Lambert & R. Oliver (Ed.), *Using tasks in second language teaching: Practice in diverse contexts* (pp. 324–343). Multilingual Matters.

Harmer, J. (2001). *The practice of English language teaching* (3rd ed.). Pearson Education.

Hassanzadeh-Taleshi, M., Yaqubi, B., & Bozorgian, H. (2021). The effects of combining task repetition with immediate post-task transcribing on L2 learners' oral narratives. *The Language*

Learning Journal. Advance online publication. https://doi.org/10.1080/09571736.2021.1901967

Hayes, J. R., & Nash, J. G. (1996). On the nature of planning in writing. In C. M. Levy & S. Ransdell (Eds.), *The science of writing* (pp. 29–56). Lawrence Erlbaum Associates.

Hedge, T. (2000). *Teaching and learning in the language classroom.* Oxford University Press.

Hegelheimer, V., & Heift, T. (2017). Computer-assisted corrective feedback and language learning. In H. Nassaji & E. Kartchava (Eds.), *Corrective feedback in second language teaching and learning* (pp. 67–81). Routledge.

Hommel. J. (2011). *The practice of English language teaching.* Longman Press.

Housen, A., Kuiken, F., & Vedder, I. (Eds.). (2012). *Dimensions of L2 performance and proficiency: Complexity, accuracy and fluency in SLA.* John Benjamins.

Hsu, H. (2012). Investigating the effects of planning on L2 chat performance. *CALICO Journal, 26,* 619–638.

Hsu, H. (2015). The effect of task planning on L2 performance and L2 development in text-based synchronous computer-mediated communication. *Applied Linguistics, 38,* 359–385.

Hsu, H. (2019). The combined effect of task repetition and post-task transcribing on L2 speaking complexity, accuracy, and fluency. *The Language Learning Journal, 47*(2), 172–187.

Inoue, C. (2016). A comparative study of the variables used to measure syntactic complexity and accuracy in task-based research. *The Language Learning Journal, 1,* 1–18.

Izumi, S. (2002). Output, input enhancement, and the Noticing Hypothesis: An experimental study on ESL relativization. *Studies in Second Language Acquisition, 24,* 541–577.

Izumi, S., & Bigelow, M. (2000). Does output promote noticing and second language acquisition? *TESOL Quarterly, 34,* 239–278.

Jackson, D. (2007). *Another look at convergent and divergent tasks: Evidence from synchronous computer-mediated communication.* Presentation at the Second International Conference on Task-Based Language Teaching, University of Hawai'i.

Jackson, D. O., & Suethanapornkul, S. (2013). The cognition hypothesis: A synthesis and meta-analysis of research on second language task complexity. *Language Learning, 63,* 330–367.

Jauregi, K. (1990). *Task-variation in native/non-native conversation*. Unpublished master's thesis, University of Reading, UK.

Johnson, M. D. (2017). Cognitive task complexity and L2 written syntactic complexity, accuracy, lexical complexity, and fluency: A research synthesis and meta-analysis. *Journal of Second Language Writing, 37*, 13–38.

Jonassen, D. H., Tessmer, M., & Hannum, W. H. (1999). *Task analysis methods for instructional design*. Lawrence Erlbaum Associates.

Kang, E., & Han, Z. (2015). The efficacy of written corrective feedback in improving L2 written accuracy: A meta-analysis. *The Modern Language Journal, 99*(1), 1–18.

Kang, S., & Lee, J.-H. (2019). Are two heads always better than one? The effects of collaborative planning on L2 writing in relation to task complexity. *Journal of Second Language Writing, 45*, 61–72.

Kartchava, E., & Nassaji, H. (2019). The role of task repetition and learner self-assessment in technology-mediated task performance. *ITL-International Journal of Applied Linguistics, 170*(2), 180–203.

Kawauchi, C. (2005). The effects of strategic planning on the oral narratives of learners with low and high intermediate L2 proficiency. In R. Ellis (Ed.), *Planning and task performance in a second language* (pp. 142–166). John Benjamins.

Keller-Lally, A. (2006). *Effect of task-type and group size on foreign language learner output in synchronous computer-mediated communication*. Unpublished PhD Thesis, University of Texas at Austin, USA.

Kellogg, R. (1996). A model of working memory in writing. In C. Levy & S. Ransdell (Eds.), *The science of writing* (pp. 57–71). Lawrence Erlbaum.

Kellogg, R. (2008). Training writing skills: A cognitive developmental perspective. *Journal of Writing Research, 1*, 1–26.

Kelly, C., & Kelly, E. (1996). *The snoop detective school conversation book*. Macmillan Language House.

Khezrlou, S. (2019a). Form-focused instruction in CALL: What do learners think? *RELC, 50*(2), 235–251.

Khezrlou, S. (2019b). Task repetition and corrective feedback: The role of feedback types and structure saliency. *English Teaching and Learning, 43*(2), 213–233.

Khezrlou, S. (2020a). The role of task repetition with direct written corrective feedback in L2 writing complexity, accuracy and fluency. *Journal of Second Language Studies, 3*(1), 31–54.

Khezrlou, S. (2020b). Training planning in second language narrative writing. *ELT Journal, 74*(1), 49–62.

Khezrlou, S. (2021a). Explicit instruction through task repetition: Effects on explicit and implicit knowledge development. *Language Awareness, 30*(1), 62–83.

Khezrlou, S. (2021b). Learners' reflective practice between the repeated performances of tasks: Effects on second language development. *Dutch Journal of Applied Linguistics, 10*, 1–20.

Khezrlou, S. (2021c). Effects of timing and availability of isolated FFI on learners' written accuracy and fluency through task repetition. *The Language Learning Journal, 49*(5), 568–580.

Khezrlou, S. (2021d). Focus on form in task repetition through oral and written task modelling. *International Review of Applied Linguistics in Language Teaching.* Advance online publication. https://doi.org/10.1515/iral-2020-0125

Khezrlou, S. (2021e). Effects of task repetition with written corrective feedback on the knowledge and written accuracy of learners with different prior knowledge of the structure. *Spanish Journal of Applied Linguistics, 34*(2), 464–493.

Khezrlou, S. (2022). Effects of task repetition with consciousness-raising in wiki-mediated collaborative writing on the development of explicit and implicit knowledge. *Computer Assisted Language Learning.* Advance online publication. https://doi.org/10.1080/09588221.2022.2033789

Khezrlou, S. (2023). Repeated academic writing with synchronous and asynchronous teacher electronic feedback: How are macro and micro aspects affected? In J. Qin & P. Stapleton (Eds.), *Using technology in second language writing: Composing, pedagogy, assessment and research*. Routledge.

Kieft, M., Rijaarsdam, G., Galbraith, D., & van den Bergh, H. (2007). The effects of adapting a writing course to students' writing strategies. *British Journal of Educational Psychology, 77*, 565–578.

Kim, Y. J. (2013). Effects of pre-task modelling on attention to form and question development. *TESOL Quarterly, 47*, 8–25.

Kim, Y. J., Choi, B., Yun, H., Kim, B., & Choi, S. (2020). Task repetition, synchronous written corrective feedback and the learning of Korean grammar: A classroom-based study. *Language Teaching Research*, 1–27.

Kim, Y. J., Kang, S., Yun, H., Kim, B., & Choi, B. (2021). The role of task repetition in a Korean as a foreign language classroom: Writing quality, attention to form, and learning of Korean grammar. *Foreign Language Annals, 53*(4), 827–849.

Kim, Y. J., & McDonough, K. (2011). Using pre-task modeling to encourage collaborative learning opportunities. *Language Teaching Research, 15*, 1–17.

Kim, Y. J., & Payant, C. (2014). A pedagogical proposal for task sequencing: An exploration of task repetition and task complexity on learning opportunities. In M. Baralt, R. Gilabert, & P. Robinson (Eds.), *Task sequencing and instructed second language learning* (pp. 151–177). Bloomsbury.

Kim, Y. J., & Payant, C. (2017). Impacts of task complexity on the development of L2 oral performance over time. *International Review of Applied Linguistics in Language Teaching, 55*(2), 197–220.

Kim, Y. J., & Tracy-Ventura, N. (2013). The role of task repetition in L2 performance development: What needs to be repeated during task-based interaction? *System, 41*, 829–840.

Kolb, D. A. (1984). *Experiential learning: Experience as the source of learning and development.* Prentice Hall.

Kolb, D. A. (2014). *Experiential learning experience as the source of learning and development.* New Jersey FT Press.

Kormos, J. (2000). The role of attention in monitoring second language speech production. *Language Learning, 50*(2), 343–384.

Kormos, J. (2006). *Speech production and second language acquisition.* Lawrence Erlbaum.

Kormos, J. (2014). Differences across modalities of performance: An investigation of linguistic and discourse complexity in narrative tasks. In H. Byrnes & R. Manchón (Eds.), *Task-based language learning—Insights from and for L2 Writing* (pp. 193–217). John Benjamins.

Kowal, M., & Swain, M. (1997). From semantic to syntactic processing: How can we promote metalinguistic awareness in the

French immersion classroom? In R. Johnson and M. Swain (Eds.), *Immersion education: international perspectives* (pp. 284–309). Cambridge University Press.

Krashen, S. (1981). Aptitude and attitude in relation to second language acquisition and learning. In K. Diller (Ed.), *Individual differences and universals in language learning aptitude* (pp. 155–175). Newbury House.

Kuiken, F., & Vedder, I. (2008). Cognitive tasks complexity and written output in Italian and French as a foreign language. *Journal of Second Language Writing, 17,* 48–60.

Lalande, J. F. (1982). Reducing composition errors: An experiment. *The Modern Language Journal, 66*(2), 140–149.

Lam, R. (2018). Promoting self-reflection in writing: A showcase portfolio approach. In A. Burns, & J. Siegel (Eds.), *International perspectives on teaching skills in ELT* (pp. 219–231). Palgrave MacMillan.

Lambert, C. (2010). A task-based needs analysis: Putting principles into practice. *Language Teaching Research, 14*(1), 99–112.

Lambert, C. (2017). Tasks, affect and second language performance. *Language Teaching Research, 21,* 657–664.

Lambert, C., Gong, Q., & Zhang, G. (2021). Learner-generated content and the lexical recall of beginning-level learners of Chinese as a Foreign Language. *Language Teaching Research.* Advance online publication. https://doi.org/10.1177/1362168820981407

Lambert, C., Kormos, J., & Minn, D. (2017). Task repetition and second language speech processing. *Studies in Second Language Acquisition, 38,* 1–30.

Lambert, C., Philp, J., & Nakamura, S. (2017). Learner-generated content and engagement in L2 task performance. *Language Teaching Research, 21,* 665–680.

Lantolf, J. (2009). Dynamic assessment: The dialectic integration of instruction and assessment. *Language Teaching, 42,* 355–368.

Larsen-Freeman, D. (2009). Adjusting expectations: The study of complexity, accuracy, and fluency in second language acquisition. *Applied Linguistics, 30*(4), 579–589.

Larsen-Freeman, D. (2012). On the roles of repetition in language teaching and learning. *Applied Linguistics Review, 3*(2), 195–210.

Lazaraton, A. (1996). Interlocutor support in oral proficiency interviews: The case of CASE. *Language Testing, 13*(2), 151–172.

Lázaro-Ibarrola, A. (2021). Model texts in collaborative and individual writing among EFL children: Noticing, incorporations, and draft quality. *International Review of Applied Linguistics in Language Teaching.* Advance online publication. https://doi.org/10.1515/iral-2020-0160

Lázaro-Ibarrola, A., & Hidalgo, M. A. (2021). Give me a second chance: Task repetition and collaborative writing with child EFL learners. *Language Teaching for Young Learners, 3*(2), 275–299.

Lee, I. (2017). Working smart or working hard: Comprehensive versus focused written corrective feedback in L2 academic contexts. In J. Bitchener, N. Storch, & R. Wette (Eds.), *Teaching writing for academic purposes to multilingual students* (pp. 168–180). Routledge.

Lee, I. (2020). Utility of focused/comprehensive written corrective feedback research for authentic L2 writing classrooms. *Journal of Second Language Writing, 49.* Advance online publication. https://doi.org/10.1016/j.jslw.2020.100734

Lee, J., & Burch, A. R. (2017). Collaborative planning in process: An ethnomethodological perspective. *TESOL Quarterly, 51,* 536–575.

Lee, M., & Révész, A. (2020). Promoting grammatical development through captions and textual enhancement in multimodal input-based tasks. *Studies in Second Language Acquisition, 42*(3), 625–651.

Levelt, W. J. (1989). *Speaking: From intention to articulation.* MIT Press.

Li, D. (2004). *The effects of pre-task planning and online planning on learners' written language performance.* Unpublished master's Thesis, the University of Auckland, New Zealand.

Li, L., Cheng, J., & Sun, L. (2015). The effects of different lengths of pretask planning time on L2 learners' oral test performance. *TESOL Quarterly, 49*(1), 38–66.

Li, S. (2010). The effectiveness of corrective feedback in SLA: A meta-analysis. *Language Learning, 60,* 309–365.

Li, S., Ellis, R., & Kim, J. (2018). The influence of pre-task grammar instruction on L2 learning: An experimental study. *Studies in English Education, 23*(4), 831–857.

Li, S., Ellis, R., & Zhu, Y. (2016). Task-based versus task-supported language instruction: An experimental study. *Annual Review of Applied Linguistics, 36*, 205–229.

Lightbown, P. M. (2000). Anniversary article. Classroom SLA research and second language teaching. *Applied linguistics, 21*(4), 431–462.

Lightbown, P. M. (2008). Transfer appropriate processing in classroom second language acquisition. In Z.-H. Han (Ed.), *Understanding second language process* (pp. 27–44). Multilingual Matters.

Lightbown, P. M., & Spada, N. (1999). *How languages are learned* (2nd ed.). Oxford University Press.

Littlewood, W. (2011). Communicative language teaching: An expanding concept for a changing world. In E. Hinkel (Ed.), *Handbook of research in second language teaching and learning* (pp. 541–557). Routledge.

Littlewood, W. (2014). Communication-oriented teaching: Where are we now? Where do we go from here? *Language Teaching, 47*, 249–362.

Loewen, S., & Nabei, T. (2007). Measuring the effects of oral corrective feedback on L2 knowledge. In A. Mackey (Ed.), *Conversational interaction in second language acquisition* (pp. 361–377). Oxford University Press.

Loewen, S., & Sato, M. (2021). Exploring the relationship between TBLT and ISLA. *TASK, 1*(1), 47–70.

Long, M. H. (1985). A role for instruction in second language acquisition: Task-based language teaching. *Modelling and Assessing Second Language Acquisition, 18*, 77–99.

Long, M. H. (1989). Task, group, and task-group interaction. *University of Hawaii Working Papers in English as a Second Language, 8*, 1–26.

Long, M. H. (1991). Focus on form in task-based language teaching. In R. Lambert & E. Shohamy (Eds.), *Language policy and pedagogy: Essays in honor of A. Ronald Walton* (pp. 179–192). John Benjamins.

Long, M. H. (1996). The role of the linguistic environment in second language acquisition. In W. C. Ritchie & T. K. Bahatia (Eds.), *Handbook of research on language acquisition* (pp. 413–468). Academic Press.

Long, M. H. (2005). Methodological issues in learner needs analysis. In M. H. Long (Ed.), *Second language needs analysis* (pp. 19–76). Cambridge University Press.

Long, M. H. (2007). Texts, tasks, and the advanced learner. In M. H. Long (Ed.), *Problems in SLA* (pp. 119–138). Lawrence Erlbaum.

Long, M. H. (2015). *Second language acquisition and task-based language teaching*. Wiley-Blackwell.

Long, M. H. (2016). In defense of tasks and TBLT: Nonissues and real issues. *Annual Review of Applied Linguistics, 36*, 5–33.

Long, M. H., & Crookes, G. (1992). Three approaches to task-based syllabus design. *TESOL Quarterly, 26*(1), 27–56.

Long, M. H., & Crookes, G. (1993). Units of analysis in syllabus design: The case for task. In G. Crookes & S. M. Gass (Eds.), *Tasks in a pedagogical context* (pp. 9–54). Multilingual Matters.

Long, M. H., & Norris, J. M. (2000). Task-based language teaching and assessment. In M. Byram (Ed.), *Encyclopedia of language teaching* (pp. 597–603). Routledge.

Loschky, L., & Bley-Vroman, R. (1993). Grammar and task-based methodology. In G. Crookes & S. Gass (Eds.), *Tasks and language learning: Integrating theory and practice* (pp. 123–167). Multilingual Matters.

Luk, J. (2010). Talking to score: Impression management in L2 oral assessment and the co-construction of a test discourse genre. *Language Assessment Quarterly, 7*(1), 25–53.

Luquin, M., & del Pilar García-Mayo, M. (2020). Collaborative writing and feedback: An exploratory study of the potential of models in primary EFL students' writing performance. *Language Teaching for Young Learners, 2*(1), 73–100.

Luquin, M., & del Pilar García-Mayo, M. (2021). Exploring the use of models as a written corrective feedback technique among EFL children. *System, 98*. Advance online publication. https://doi.org/10.1016/j.system.2021.102465

Lynch, T. (2001). Seeing what they meant: Transcribing as a route to noticing. *ELT Journal, 55*(2), 124–132.

Lynch, T. (2007). Learning from the transcripts of an oral communication task. *ELT Journal, 61*(4), 311–320.

Lynch, T. (2018). Enhancing task repetition in second language speaking classes. In M. Bygate (Ed.), *Learning language through task repetition* (pp. 193–222). John Benjamins.

Lynch, T., & Maclean, J. (2000). Exploring the benefits of task repetition and recycling for classroom language learning. *Language Teaching Research, 4,* 221–250.

Lynch, T., & Maclean, J. (2001). Effects of immediate task repetition on learners' performance. In M. Bygate, P. Skehan, & M. Swain (Eds.), *Researching pedagogic tasks, second language learning, teaching and testing* (pp. 141–163). Longman.

Lyster, R. (2001). Negotiation of form, recasts, and explicit correction in relation to error types and learner repair in immersion classrooms. *Language Learning, 51,* 265–301.

Lyster, R., & Ranta, L. (1997). Corrective feedback and learner uptake. *Studies in Second Language Acquisition, 19,* 37–66.

Lyster, R., & Ranta, L. (2013) Counterpoint piece: The case for variety in corrective feedback research. *Studies in Second Language Acquisition, 35*(1), 167–184.

Lyster, R., & Saito, K. (2010). Oral feedback in classroom SLA: A meta-analysis. *Studies in Second Language Acquisition, 32,* 265–302.

Mackay, R. (1978). Identifying the nature of the learner's needs. In R. Mackay & A. Mountford (Eds.), *English for specific purposes* (pp. 21–42). Longman.

Mackey, A. (1999). Input, interaction, and second language development. *Studies in Second Language Acquisition, 21*(4), 557–587.

Mackey, A. (2012). *Input, interaction and corrective feedback in L2 classroom.* Oxford University Press.

Malicka, A., & Sasayama, S. (2017). *The importance of learning from the accumulated knowledge: Findings from a research synthesis on task complexity.* Paper presented at the 7th Biennial International Conference on Task-Based Language Teaching, Barcelona, Spain.

Manchon, R. M. (2014). The distinctive nature of task repetition writing: Implications for theory, research and pedagogy. *Estudios de Lingüística Inglesa Aplicada, 14,* 13–41.

Mehnert, U. (1998). The effects of different lengths of time for planning on second language performance. *Studies in Second Language Acquisition, 20*(1), 83–108.

Mennim, P. (2003). Rehearsed oral L2 output and reactive focus on form. *ELT Journal, 57*(2), 130–138.

Michel, M. (2011). Effects of task complexity and interaction on L2 performance. In P. Robinson (Ed.), *Second language task complexity: Researching the Cognition Hypothesis of language learning and performance* (pp. 141–174). John Benjamins.

Michel, M. C., Kuiken, F., & Vedder, I. (2012). Task complexity and interaction: (Combined) effects on task-based performance in Dutch as a second language. *EUROSLA Yearbook, 12*(1), 164–190.

Mislevy, R. J. (2010). Some implications of expertise research for educational assessment. *Research Papers in Education, 25*(3), 253–270.

Mislevy, R. J., Steinberg, L. S., & Almond, R. A. (2002). Design and analysis in task-based language assessment. *Language Assessment, 19*, 477–496.

Moon, J. A. (2004). *A handbook of reflective and experiential learning*. Routledge.

Nakahama, Y., Tyler, A., & van Lier, L. (2001). Negotiation of meaning in conversational and information gap activities: a comparative discourse analysis. *TESOL Quarterly, 35*(3), 377–405.

Nakatsuhara, F. (2004). *An investigation into conversation styles in paired speaking tests.* Unpublished master's thesis, University of Essex, Essex, UK.

Nassaji, H. (2016). Anniversary article: Interactional feedback in second language teaching and
learning: A synthesis and analysis of current research. *Language Teaching Research, 20,* 535–562.

Newell, A., & Simon, H. A. (1972). *Human problem solving.* Prentice-Hall, INC.

Ng, C., & Tang, E. (1997). Teachers' needs in the process of EFL reform in China: A report from Shanghai. *Perspective, 9,* 63–85.

Nitta, R., & Baba, K. (2014). Task repetition and L2 writing development. In H. Byrnes & R. M. Manchón (Eds.), *Task-based language learning. Insights from and for L2 writing* (pp. 107–136). John Benjamins.

Nitta, R., & Baba, K. (2018). Understanding the benefits of repetition from a complex dynamic systems perspective: The case of a writing task. In M. Bygate (Ed.), *Learning language through task repetition* (pp. 285–316). John Benjamins.

Nitta, R., & Nakatsuhara, F. (2014). A multifaceted approach to investigating pre-task planning effects on oral task performance. *Language Testing, 31*(2), 147–175.

Niwa, Y. (2000). *Reasoning demands of L2 tasks and L2 narrative production: Effects of individual differences in working memory, intelligence, and aptitude.* Unpublished master's thesis, Aoyama Gakuin University, Tokyo.

Norris, J. M. (2000). Purposeful language assessment. *English Teaching Forum, 38*(1), 18–23.

Norris, J. M. (2002). Interpretations, intended uses and designs in task-based language assessment. *Language Testing, 19*(4), 337–346.

Norris, J. M. (2006). The issue: The why (and how) of assessing student learning outcomes in college foreign language programs. *The Modern Language Journal, 90*(4), 576–583.

Norris, J. M. (2009). Task-based teaching and testing. In M. H. Long & C. J. Doughty (Eds.), *Handbook of language teaching* (pp. 578–594). Blackwell.

Norris, J. M. (2016). Current uses for task-based language assessment. *Annual Review of Applied Linguistics, 36*, 230–244.

Norris, J. M. (2018). Task-based language assessment: Aligning designs with intended uses and consequences. *JLTA Journal, 21*, 3–20.

Norris, J. M., Brown, J. D., Hudson, T., & Yoshioka, J. (1998). *Designing second language performance assessments.* University of Hawai'i Press.

Nunan, D. (1989). *Designing tasks for the communicative classroom.* Cambridge University Press.

Nunan, D. (1991). Communicative tasks and the language curriculum. *TESOL Quarterly, 25*(2), 279–295.

Nunan, D. (2004). *Task-based language teaching.* Cambridge University Press.

O'Grady, S. (2019). The impact of pre-task planning on speaking test performance for English-medium university admission. *Language Teaching Research, 36*(4), 505–526.

Ortega, L. (1999). Planning and focus on form in L2 oral performance. *Studies in Second Language Acquisition, 21*, 109–48.

Ortega, L. (2005). What do learners plan? Learner-driven attention to form during pre-task planning. In R. Ellis (Ed.), *Planning and task performance in a second language* (pp. 77–109). John Benjamins.

O'Sullivan, B. (2012). Assessing speaking. In C. Coombe, P. Davidson, B. O'Sullivan & S. Stoynoff (Eds.), *The Cambridge guide to second language assessment* (pp. 234–247). Cambridge University Press.

Pang, F., & Skehan, P. (2014). Self-reported planning behavior and second language performance in narrative retelling. In P. Skehan (Ed.), *Processing perspectives on task performance* (pp. 95–127). John Benjamins.

Patanasorn, C. (2010). *Effects of procedural content and task repetition on accuracy and fluency in an EFL context.* Northern Arizona University.

Pellegrino, J. W., Chudowsky, N., & Glaser, R. (Eds.). (2001). *Knowing what students know: The science and design of educational assessment.* National Academies Press.

Pellegrino, J. W., & Wilson, M. (2015). Assessment of complex cognition: Commentary on the design and validation of assessments. *Theory into Practice, 54*(3), 263–273.

Pellicer- Sánchez, A. (2016). Incidental L2 vocabulary acquisition from and while reading. *Studies in Second Language Acquisition, 38*(1), 97–130.

Philp, J., & Duchesne, S. (2016). Exploring engagement in tasks in the language classroom. *Annual Review of Applied Linguistics, 36,* 50–72.

Pica, T. (1987). Second language acquisition, social interaction and the classroom. *Applied Linguistics, 81,* 3–21.

Pica, T., Kanagy R., & Falodun, J. (1993). Choosing and using communication tasks for second language instruction and research. In G. Crookes & S. M. Gass (Eds.), *Tasks and language learning: Integrating theory and practice* (pp. 9–34). Multilingual Matters.

Pienemann, M. (1985). Learnability and syllabus construction. In K. Hyltenstam & M. Pienemann (Eds.), *Modelling and assessing second language acquisition* (pp. 23–75). Multilingual Matters.

Pintrich, P. (2000). The role of goal orientation in self-regulated learning. In M. Boekaerts and P. Pintrich (Eds.), *Handbook of self-regulation* (pp. 452–502). Elsevier Academic Press.

Poehner, M. E. (2018). Probing and provoking L2 development: The object of mediation in dynamic assessment and mediated development. In J. P. Lantolf, M. E. Poehner & M. Swain (Eds.), *The Routledge handbook of sociocultural theory and second language development* (pp. 249–265). Routledge.

Polio, C. (2012). The relevance of second language acquisition theory to the written error correction debate. *Journal of Second Language Writing, 21,* 375–389.

Prabhu, N. S. (1987). *Second language pedagogy.* Oxford University Press.

Puimège, E., Montero Perez, M., & Peters, E. (2021). Promoting L2 acquisition of multiword units through textually enhanced audiovisual input: an eye-tracking study. *Second Language Research.* Advance online publication. https://doi.org/10.1177/02676583211049741

Qian, L. (2014). The effects of post-task transcribing on learners' oral performance. In P. Skehan (Ed.), *Processing perspectives on task performance* (pp. 129–154). John Benjamins.

Qin, J. (2008). The effect of processing instruction and dictogloss tasks on acquisition of the English passive voice. *Language Teaching Research, 12*(1), 61–82.

Qin, J., & Zhang, Y. (2019). Pre-task planning and discourse cohesion: Analysis of Chinese EFL learners' referential use in oral narratives. *Language Teaching Research.* Advance online publication. https://doi.org/10.1177/1362168819883896

Rahimi, M. (2021). A comparative study of the impact of focused vs. comprehensive corrective feedback and revision on ESL learners' writing accuracy and quality. *Language Teaching Research, 25*(5), 687–710.

Richards, J., & Rodgers, T. (2001). *Approaches and methods in language teaching.* Cambridge University Press.

Richards, J. C., Platt, J., & Weber, H. (1985). *Dictionary of applied linguistics.* Longman.

Richards, J., & Schmidt, R. (2010). *Longman dictionary of language teaching and applied linguistics* (4th ed.). Longman.

Richterich, R. (1983). *Case studies in identifying language needs*. Pergamon Press.

Robb, T., Ross, S., & Shortreed, I. (1986). Salience of feedback on error and its effect on EFL writing quality. *TESOL Quarterly, 20*(1), 83–95.

Robinson, P. (1996). Task-based testing, performance-referencing and program development. *University of Queensland Working Papers in Language and Linguistics, 1*(1), 95–116.

Robinson, P. (2001a). Task complexity, task difficulty, and task production: Exploring interactions in a componential framework. *Applied Linguistics, 22*(1), 27–57.

Robinson, P. (2001b). Task complexity, cognitive resources, and syllabus design: A triadic framework for examining task influences on SLA. In P. Robinson (Ed.), *Cognition and second language instruction* (pp. 287–318). Cambridge University Press.

Robinson, P. (2003). Attention and memory during SLA. In C. Doughty & M.H. Long (Eds.), *Handbook of second language acquisition* (pp. 631–678). Blackwell.

Robinson, P. (2005). Cognitive complexity and task sequencing: Studies in a componential framework for second language task design. *International Review of Applied Linguistics in Language Teaching, 43*(1), 1–32.

Robinson, P. (2007). Criteria for classifying and sequencing pedagogic tasks. In M. P. Garcia Mayo (Ed.), *Investigating tasks in formal language learning* (pp. 7–26). Multilingual Matters.

Robinson, P. (2010). Situating and distributing cognition. Across task demands: The SSARC model of pedagogic task sequencing. In M. Putz & L. Sicola (Eds.), *Cognitive processing in second language acquisition: Inside the learner's mind* (pp. 243–268). John Benjamins.

Robinson, P. (2011a). Second language task complexity, the cognition hypothesis, language learning, and performance. In P. Robinson (Ed.), *Second language task complexity: Researching the cognition hypothesis on language learning and performance* (pp. 3–37). John Benjamins.

Robinson, P. (2011b). Task based language learning: A review of issues. *Language Learning, 61*(1), 1–36.

Robinson, P., & Gilabert, R. (2007). Task complexity, the Cognition Hypothesis and second language learning and performance.

International Review of Applied Linguistics in Language Teaching 45(3), 161–76.

Robinson, P., & Ross, S. (1996). The development of task-based assessment in English for academic purpose programs. *Applied Linguistics, 17*, 455–76.

Rogers, J. (2015). Learning second language syntax under massed and distributed conditions. *TESOL Quarterly, 49*, 857–866.

Rohrer, D., & Pashler, H. (2007). Increasing retention without increasing study time. *Current Directions in Psychological Science, 16*, 183–186.

Rost, M. (2011). *Teaching and researching listening: Applied linguistics in action*. Pearson Education.

Rostamian, M., Fazilatfar, A. M., & Jabbari, A. A. (2017). The effect of planning time on cognitive processes, monitoring behavior, and quality of L2 writing. *Language Teaching Research, 22*(4), 418–438.

Sadeghi, M., & Pourhaji, M. (2021). The effects of pre-task explicit instruction on L2 oral self-repair behavior. *Language Teaching Research*. Advance online publication. https://doi.org/10.1177/13621688211048766

Sample, E., & Michel, M. (2014). An exploratory study into trade-off effects of complexity, accuracy, and fluency on young learners' oral task repetition. *TESL Canada Journal, 31*, 23–46.

Samuda, V. (2001). Guiding relationships between form and meaning during task performance: The role of the teacher. In M. Bygate, P. Skehan & M. Swain (Eds.), *Researching pedagogic tasks: Second language learning, teaching and testing* (pp. 119–140). Longman.

Samuda, V., & Bygate, M. (2008). *Tasks in second language learning*. Palgrave Macmillan.

Sánchez, A. J., Manchón, R. M., & Gilabert, R. (2020). The effects of task repetition across modalities and proficiency levels. In R. M Manchón (Ed.), *Writing and language learning: Advancing research agendas* (pp. 121–143). John Benjamins.

Sangarun, J. (2005). The effects of focusing on meaning and form in strategic planning. In R. Ellis (Ed.), *Planning and task performance in a second language* (pp. 111–142). John Benjamins.

Sato, M. (2020). Metacognitive instruction for collaborative interaction: The process and product of self-regulated learning in the Chilean EFL context. In C. Lambert & R. Oliver (Eds.), *Using tasks in diverse contexts* (pp. 149–171). Multilingual Matters.

Schmidt, R. (1990). The role of consciousness in second language learning. *Applied Linguistics, 11*, 129–58.

Schildkamp, K., van der Kleij, F. M., Heitink, M. C., Kippers, W. B., & Veldkamp, B. P. (2020). Formative assessment: A systematic review of critical teacher prerequisites for classroom practice. *International Journal of Educational Research, 103*. Advance online publication. https://doi.org/10.1016/j.ijer.2020.101602

Schon, D. (2016). *The reflective practitioner: How professionals think in action*. Routledge.

Sheen, Y. (2007). The effects of corrective feedback, language aptitude, and learner attitudes on the acquisition of English articles. In A. Mackey (Ed.), *Conversational interaction in second language acquisition* (pp. 301–322). Oxford University Press.

Sheen, Y., Wright, D., & Moldawa, A. (2009). Differential effects of focused and unfocused written correction on the accurate use of grammatical forms by adult ESL learners. *System, 37*(4), 556–569.

Shehadeh, A. (2012). Broadening the perspective of task-based language teaching scholarship: The contribution of research in foreign language contexts. In A. Shehadeh & C. A. Coombe (Eds.), *Task-based language teaching in foreign language contexts: Research and implementation* (pp. 1–20). John Benjamins.

Sheppard, C. (2006). *The effects of instruction directed at the gaps second language learners noticed in their oral production*. Unpublished PhD Thesis, University of Auckland, New Zealand.

Sheppard, C., & Ellis, R. (2018). The effects of awareness-raising through stimulated recall on the repeated performance of the same task and on a new task of the same type. In M. Bygate (Ed.), *Learning language through task repetition* (pp. 177–199). John Benjamins.

Shintani, N. (2017). The effects of the timing of isolated FFI on the explicit knowledge and written accuracy of learners with different prior knowledge of the linguistic target. *Studies in Second Language Acquisition, 39*(1), 129–166.

Shintani, N., Aubrey, S., & Donnellan, M. (2016). The effects of pre-task and post-task metalinguistic explanations on accuracy in second language writing. *TESOL Quarterly, 50*(4), 945–954.

Shintani, N., & Ellis, R. (2013). The comparative effect of direct written corrective feedback and metalinguistic explanation on learners' explicit and implicit knowledge of the English indefinite article. *Journal of Second Language Writing, 22,* 286–306.

Shintani, N., Ellis, R., & Suzuki, W. (2014). Effects of written feedback and revision on learners' accuracy in using two English grammatical structures. *Language Learning, 64,* 103–131.

Simon, H. A. (1978). Information-processing theory of human problem solving. In W. K. Estes (Ed.), *Handbook of learning and cognition processes* (pp. 271–295). Erlbaum Associates.

Skehan, P. (1996). A framework for the implementation of task-based instruction. *Applied Linguistics, 17*(1), 38–62.

Skehan, P. (1998). *A cognitive approach to language learning.* Oxford University Press.

Skehan, P. (2001). A framework for implementation of task-based instruction. *Applied Linguistics, 17,* 38–62.

Skehan, P. (2002). Theorizing and updating aptitude. In P. Robinson (Ed.), *Individual differences and instructed language learning* (pp. 69–94). John Benjamins.

Skehan, P. (2003). Task-based instruction. *Language Teaching, 36,* 1–14.

Skehan, P. (2009). Modelling second language performance: Integrating complexity, accuracy, fluency, and lexis. *Applied Linguistics, 30*(4), 510–532.

Skehan, P. (2014). *Processing perspectives on task performance.* John Benjamins.

Skehan, P. (2016). Tasks vs. conditions: Two perspectives on task research and its implications for pedagogy. *Annual Review of Applied Linguistics, 36,* 34–49.

Skehan, P. (2018a). *Second language task-based performance: Theory, research, and assessment.* Routledge.

Skehan, P. (2018b). *The story of planning: 1987-2017* [Paper presentation]. Birkbeck University, London, England.

Skehan, P., & Foster, P. (1997). The influence of planning and post-task activities on accuracy and complexity in task-based learning. *Language Teaching Research, 1,* 185–211.

Skehan, P., & Foster, P. (1999). The influence of task structure and processing conditions on narrative retellings. *Language Learning, 49*(1), 93–120.

Skehan, P., & Foster, P. (2001). Cognition and tasks. In P. Robinson (Ed.), *Cognition and second language instruction* (pp. 183–205). Cambridge University Press.

Skehan, P., & Foster, P. (2005). Strategic and on-line planning. In R. Ellis (Ed.), *Planning and task performance in a second language* (pp. 193–216). John Benjamins.

Skehan, P., & Foster, P. (2007). Complexity, accuracy, fluency, and lexis in task-based performance: A meta-analysis of the Ealing Research. In S. van Daele, A. Housen, F. Kuiken, M. Pierrard, & I. Vedder (Eds.), *Complexity, accuracy, and fluency in second language use, learning, and teaching* (pp. 207–226). KVAB.

Skehan, P., Xiaoyue, B., Qian, L., & Wang, Z. (2012). The task is not enough: Processing approaches to task-based performance. *Language Teaching Research 16*, 170–87.

Slimani-Rolls, A. (2005). Rethinking task-based language learning: what we can learn from the learners. *Language Teaching Research, 9*(2), 195–218.

Svalberg, A. (2012). Language awareness in language learning and teaching: A research agenda. *Language Teaching, 45*(3), 376–388.

Suzuki, Y. (2017). The optimal distribution of practice for the acquisition of L2 morphology: A conceptual replication and extension. *Language Learning, 67*, 512–545.

Suzuki, Y., & DeKeyser, R. (2017). Effects of distributed practice on the proceduralization of morphology. *Language Teaching Research, 21*, 166–188.

Stillwell, C., Curabba, B., Alexander, K., Kidd, A., Kim, E., Stone, P., & Wyle, C. (2010). Students transcribing tasks: Noticing fluency, accuracy, and complexity. *ELT Journal, 64*(4), 445–55.

Svalberg, A. M.-L., & Askham, J. (2020). Teacher and learner perceptions of adult foreign language learners' engagement with consciousness-raising tasks in four languages. *Language Awareness, 29*(3-4), 236–254.

Swain, M. (1985). Large scale communicative testing: A case study. In Y. Lee, C. Fok, R. Lord & G. Low (Eds.), *New directions in language testing* (pp. 35–46). Pergamon Press.

Swain. M. (1998). Focus on form through conscious reflection. In C. Doughty & J. Williams (Eds.), *Focus on form in classroom second language acquisition* (pp.64–81). Cambridge University Press.

Swain, M. (2005). The output hypothesis: Theory and research. In E. Hinkel (Ed.), *Handbook on research in second language teaching and learning* (pp. 87–101). Lawrence Erlbaum.

Swain, M., & Lapkin, S. (1995). Problems in output and the cognitive processes they generate: A step towards second language learning. *Applied Linguistics, 16*, 371–391.

Swain, M., & Lapkin, S. (1998). Interaction and second language learning: Two adolescent French immersion students working together. *Modern Language Journal, 82*, 320–37.

Swain, M., & Lapkin, S. (2001). Focus on form through collaborative dialogue: Exploring task effects. In M. Bygate, P. Skehan & M. Swain (Eds.), *Researching pedagogical tasks: Second language learning, teaching and testing* (pp. 99–118). Longman.

Swan, M. (2005). Legislation by hypothesis: The case of task-based instruction. *Applied Linguistics, 26*, 376–401.

Tarone, E. (1983). On the variability of interlanguage systems. *Applied Linguistics, 4*, 143–163.

Tarone, E., & Yule, G. (1989). *Focus on the language learner: Approaches to identifying and meeting the needs of second language learners*. Oxford University Press.

Tavakoli, P. (2016). Fluency in monologic and dialogic task performance: Challenges in defining and measuring L2 fluency. *International Review of Applied Linguistics in Language Teaching, 54*(2), 133–150.

Tavakoli, P., & Foster, P. (2008). Task design and L2 performance. *Language Learning, 58*(2), 429–473.

Teng, L. S., & Zhang, L. J. (2016). A questionnaire-based validation of multidimensional models of self-regulated learning strategies. *Modern Language Journal, 100*, 674–701.

Thai, C., & Boers, F. (2016). Repeating a monologue under increasing time pressure: Effects on fluency, complexity, and accuracy. *TESOL Quarterly, 50*(2), 369–393.

Timpe-Laughlin, V. (2018). Pragmatics in task-based language assessment: Opportunities and challenges. In N. Taguchi & Y. Kim (Eds.), *Task-based approaches to teaching and assessing pragmatics* (pp. 287–304). John Benjamins.

Truscott, J. (1996). The case against grammar correction in L2 writing classes. *Language learning, 46,* 327–369.
Ur, P. (1996). *A course in language teaching: Practice and theory.* Cambridge University Press.
Van Beuningen, C. G., De Jong, N. H., & Kuiken, F. (2012). Evidence on the effectiveness of comprehensive error correction in second language writing. *Language Learning, 62*(1), 1–41.
Van de Guchte, M., Braaksma, M., Rojlaarsdam, G., & Bimmel, P. (2016). Focus on form through task repetition in TBLT. *Language Teaching Research, 20*(3), 300–320.
Van de Guchte, M., Rijlaarsdam, G., Braaksma, M., & Bimmel, P. (2017). Focus on language versus content in the pre-task: Effects of guided peer-video model observations on task performance. *Language Teaching Research, 23*(3), 310–329.
Van den Branden, K. (2016). The role of teachers in task-based language education. *Annual Review of Applied Linguistics, 36,* 164–181.
Van den Branden, K., Bygate, M., & Norris, J. M. (2009). *Task-based language teaching: A reader.* John Benjamins.
Van Gorp, K., & Deygers, B. (2013). Task-based language assessment. In A. J. Kunnan (Ed.), *The companion to language assessment: Approaches and development* (pp. 578–593). Wiley.
Varonis, E., & Gass, S. M. (1985). Non-native/non-native conversations: A model for negotiation of meaning. *Applied Linguistics, 6,* 71–90.
Vygotsky, L. S. (1978). *Mind in society: The development of higher psychological processes.* MIT Press.
Wang, G., & Wang, S.-D. (2014). Explicit grammar instruction for EFL writing and editing: An exploratory study at a Korean university. *Linguistics and Literature Studies, 2,* 65–73.
Wang Z. (2014). On-line time pressure manipulations: L2 speaking performance under five types of planning and repetition conditions. In P. Skehan (Ed.), *Processing perspectives on task performance* (pp. 27–62). John Benjamins.
Weaver, C. (2013). Incorporating a formative assessment cycle into task-based language teaching. In A. Shehadeh & C. Coombe (Eds.), *Researching and implementing task-based language learning and teaching in EFL contexts* (pp. 287–312). John Benjamins.

Webber, B. (2008). Computational perspectives on discourse and dialogue. In D. Schiffrin, D. Tannen & H. Hamilton (Eds.), *The handbook of discourse analysis* (pp. 798–817). Routledge.

Wegerif, R., Mercer, N., Dawes, L. (1999). From social interaction to individual reasoning: An empirical investigation of a possible sociocultural model of cognitive development. *Learning and Instruction, 9*, 493–516.

Wendel, J. N. (1997). *Planning and second language narrative production*. Unpublished PhD Thesis, Temple University, Japan.

Wenden, A. L. (1987). Conceptual background and utility. In A. L. Wenden and J. Rubin (Eds.), *Learner strategies in language learning* (pp. 3–13). Prentice-Hall.

Wertsch, J. V. (1985). *Voices of the mind: A sociocultural approach to mediated action*. Harvard University Press.

Westwood, P. S. (2016). *Reading and learning difficulties: Approaches to teaching and assessment*. Victoria ACER Press.

Widdowson, H.G. (1990). *Aspects of language teaching*. Oxford University Press.

Wiener, S., Ito, K., & Speer, S. (2021). Effects of multitalker input and instructional method on the dimension-based statistical learning of syllable-tone combinations: An eye-tracking study. *Studies in Second Language Acquisition, 43*(1), 155–180.

Wigglesworth, G. (1997). An investigation of planning time and proficiency level on oral test discourse. *Language Testing, 14*(1), 85–106.

Wigglesworth, G. (2001). Influences on performance in task-based oral assessments. In M. Bygate, P. Skehan, & M. Swain (Eds.), *Researching pedagogic tasks: Second language learning, teaching, and testing* (pp. 186–209). Longman.

Wiliam, D. (2011). What is assessment for learning? *Studies in Educational Evaluation, 37*, 3–14.

Wilkins, D. (1976). *Notional syllabuses*. Oxford University Press.

Willis, D., & Willis, J. (2007). *Doing task-based teaching*. Oxford University Press.

Willis, J. (1996). *A framework for task-based learning*. Longman.

Willis, J., & Willis, D. (1988). *COBUILD English course*. Collins.

Winke, P. (2014). Formative, task-based oral assessments in an advanced Chinese language class. In M. González-Lloret & L.

Ortega (Eds.), *Technology-mediated TBLT: Researching technology and tasks* (pp. 264–293). John Benjamins.

Witkin, B. R., & Altschuld, J. W. (1995). *Planning and conducting needs assessments: A practical guide*. Sage.

Wolf, M. K., Lopez, A., Oh, S., & Tsutagawa, F. S. (2017). Comparing the performance of young English language learners and native English speakers on speaking assessment tasks. In M. Wolf & Y. Butler (Eds.), *English language proficiency assessments for young learners* (pp. 171–190). Routledge.

Yang, L., & Zhang, L. (2010). Exploring the role of reformulations and a model text in EFL students' writing performance. *Language Teaching Research, 14*(4), 464–484.

Yannakoudakis, H., Andersen, Ø. E., Geranpayeh, A., Briscoe, T., & Nicholls, D. (2018). Developing an automated writing placement system for ESL learners. *Applied Measurement in Education, 31*(3), 251–267.

Yilmaz, Y. (2012). The relative effects of explicit correction and recasts on two target structures via two communication modes. *Language Learning, 6,* 1134–1169.

Yilmaz, Y., & Granena, G. (2016). The role of cognitive aptitudes for explicit language learning in the relative effects of explicit and implicit feedback. *Bilingualism: Language and Cognition, 19*(1), 147–161.

Yoshida, R. (2010). How do teachers and learners perceive corrective feedback in the Japanese language classroom? *The Modern Language Journal, 94,* 293–314.

Youn, S. J. (2015). Validity argument for assessing L2 pragmatics in interaction using mixed methods. *Language Testing, 32*(2), 199–225.

Youn, S. J. (2018). Task-based needs analysis of L2 pragmatics in an EAP context. *Journal of English for Academic Purposes, 36,* 86–98.

Yuan, F., & Ellis, R. (2003). The effects of pre-task planning and online planning on fluency, complexity, and accuracy in L2 monologic oral production. *Applied Linguistics, 24*(1), 1–27

Zalbidea, J. (2021). On the scope of output in SLA: Task modality, salience, L2 grammar noticing, and development. *Studies in Second Language Acquisition, 43*(1), 50–82.

Zhang, X., & Lantolf, J. (2015). Natural or artificial: Is the route of L2 development teachable? *Language Learning, 65*, 152–180.

Zhu, M., Liu, O. L., & Lee, H. S. (2020). The effect of automated feedback on revision behavior and learning gains in formative assessment of scientific argument writing. *Computers & Education, 143*, 103668. Advance online publication. https://doi.org/10.1016/j.compedu.2019.103668

Index

accuracy, 24, 28, 36, 43, 49, 50, 52, 53, 54, 55, 56, 65, 67, 69, 70, 73, 74, 75, 81, 82, 83, 84, 86, 87, 88, 89, 90, 91, 92, 93, 94, 97, 98, 99, 100, 101, 103, 105, 106, 108, 109, 111, 114, 116, 117, 119, 121
aptitude, 36, 37, 39, 41, 48, 75
attention, 5, 7, 8, 20, 21, 22, 23, 26, 27, 36, 38, 46, 49, 50, 51, 52, 53, 54, 55, 61, 64, 66, 67, 68, 69, 70, 71, 72, 74, 75, 76, 77, 78, 80, 81, 82, 83, 86, 89, 90, 94, 98, 99, 104, 106, 107, 108, 110, 111, 113, 114, 115, 118, 121, 122. 125, 133, 134, 139, 141, 144
attentional resources, 49, 52, 81, 82, 89, 94, 98
automatize, 39, 56, 63, 86, 92
Bangalore project, 31, 32, 43, 44
cognition hypothesis, 51, 55, 98
cognitive-interactionist, 5, 65
communicative language teaching, 4, 31
competence, 4, 32, 38, 40, 121, 127, 132, 143

complexity, 36, 42, 50, 52, 55, 56, 67, 69, 70, 74, 84, 86, 87, 89, 90, 91, 93, 97, 98, 99, 100, 101, 103, 104, 106, 108, 109, 111
complexity, accuracy, fluency/CAF, 49, 50, 51, 81, 83, 90, 91, 93, 94, 97, 98, 99, 103, 105, 106, 108, 109, 111, 140
computer, 133, 146, 157, 158, 159, 179
consciousness-raising task, 22, 74, 76, 113
content-based language teaching/CLIL, 38
corrective feedback, 7, 71, 72, 89, 91, 107, 114, 115, 120, 122
explicit, 5, 7, 22, 39, 40, 45, 52, 61, 62, 63, 64, 65, 67, 68, 69, 70, 71, 72, 73, 74, 75, 76, 77, 92, 104, 113, 115, 117, 118, 121, 140, 141, 142
fluency, 36, 73, 89, 90, 92, 109
focus on form/FonF, 61, 62, 66, 67, 68, 69, 70, 71, 72, 73, 74, 76, 77
formative, 8, 85, 126, 132, 134, 135, 143, 144

Index

form-focused, 7, 61, 61, 67, 76, 77, 90, 93
grading, 6, 34, 44, 48, 49, 50
grammar, 21, 38, 42, 47, 63, 64, 65, 68, 69, 70, 91, 103, 108, 111, 119, 134, 141
implementation, 3, 5, 6, 7, 8, 31, 49, 50, 51, 57, 59, 63, 78, 81, 93, 125, 127, 129, 130, 135, 136, 139, 140, 141, 143, 144, 145
implicit, 39, 64, 69, 71, 72, 75, 76, 92, 113, 115, 117, 118, 120, 140, 142
incidental, 47, 62, 65, 71
individual difference, 23, 36, 37, 38
information-gap, 25, 29, 44, 126
intentional, 31, 65, 71
interaction, 3, 5, 18, 19, 20, 22, 24, 25, 26, 27, 28, 29, 30, 35, 39, 46, 65, 82, 83, 100, 112, 113, 114, 115, 120, 121, 134
interaction hypothesis, 71, 120
language related episodes/LREs, 83, 84, 114
lexis, 4, 32, 90, 111
lexical complexity, 28, 55, 89, 90
limited capacity model/LCM, 7, 49, 61, 63, 81, 98
measurement, 8, 125, 131, 132, 133, 134, 136, 144
modular, 7, 39, 40, 66, 75, 76, 77, 142

motivation, 5, 36, 37, 39, 41, 48, 140
narrative task, 22, 24, 49, 68, 74, 75, 91, 92, 101, 108, 111, 114
needs analysis, 6, 33, 34, 35, 38, 40, 46, 129, 133, 139
negotiation of meaning, 19, 25, 26, 48, 71
noticing, 4, 20, 21, 28, 66, 74, 109, 110, 111, 112, 115
on-line planning, 95, 99, 100, 101
opinion-gap task, 23, 26, 29, 44, 68, 85, 126
output, 6, 7, 17, 19, 20, 21, 22, 26, 27, 28, 35, 37, 47, 71, 78, 89, 95, 100, 108, 115, 142
pedagogic task, 6, 16, 17, 19, 28, 30, 32, 33, 34, 42, 43, 45, 46, 64
planning, 7, 27, 31, 47, 50, 52, 53, 54, 56, 64, 65, 67, 70, 80, 88, 89, 94, 95, 96, 97, 98, 99, 100, 101, 102, 103, 104, 105, 106, 110, 119, 129, 130, 140, 141
post-task, 7, 47, 50, 51, 61, 62, 66, 69, 73, 74, 107, 108, 109, 122, 140, 143, 144
pragmatics, 21, 47, 133
presentation–practice–production/PPP, 76, 89, 91, 153, 154
pre-task, 7, 47, 50, 61, 62, 63, 64, 66, 67, 68, 69, 70, 77, 94, 96, 97, 98, 99, 100, 101,

102, 103, 104, 105, 110, 130, 140, 141, 143
qualitative, 57, 66, 86, 104, 131, 136, 144
quantitative, 57, 66, 131
rating, 62, 69, 78, 84, 86, 92, 94, 99, 103, 105, 111, 125, 126, 129, 130, 131, 132, 133, 136, 143
real-world, 4, 6, 14, 16, 18, 19, 33, 40, 46, 125, 126, 127, 128, 132, 139
reasoning, 37, 43, 44, 46, 49, 51, 52, 55, 64, 81, 118, 126
recasts, 71, 72, 117
repair, 28, 87, 109, 111, 116
repetition, 7, 51, 54, 74, 78, 79, 80, 81, 82, 83, 84, 85, 86, 87, 88, 89, 90, 91, 92, 93, 96, 107, 108, 140
second language acquisition/SLA, 4, 5, 20, 34, 54, 56, 64, 65, 72, 73, 75, 76, 85, 88, 101, 106, 108, 109, 110, 115, 120, 121, 130, 140
sequencing, 6, 31, 35, 36, 42, 43, 45, 46, 47, 48, 49, 51, 53, 54, 55, 56, 57, 129, 139
skill acquisition theory, 74, 75, 76, 97, 98, 127, 132, 164
sociocultural theory, 65, 115
speaking, 7, 21, 44, 50, 88, 89, 90, 102, 103, 108, 111, 119, 130, 131, 132, 134
SSARC, 51, 52, 53, 56
stimulated recall, 91, 101
subordination, 92, 97, 111
summative test, 126

syntactic complexity, 42, 49, 55, 70, 81, 89, 97, 101
task as workplan, 18, 38, 57, 62, 139
task complexity, 42, 43, 44, 45, 47, 49, 51, 53, 55, 57
task design, 31, 127, 128, 139
task modeling, 109, 111
task planning, 94, 95, 96, 100, 103, 104
task repetition, 78, 79, 81, 82, 83, 85, 87, 89, 91, 93
task selection, 30, 31, 32, 33, 35, 37, 38, 39, 40, 41
task sequencing, 43, 45, 47, 49, 51, 53, 55, 57
task type, 15, 23
task-based language assessment/TBLA, 5, 8, 125, 126, 127, 131, 132, 133, 134, 135, 136, 143, 144
task-supported language teaching/TSLT, 47, 61, 62, 63, 64, 65, 72, 75, 76, 80
technology, 91, 125, 133, 143
trade-off, 7, 36, 49, 55, 81, 98, 99
Triadic Componential Framework/TCF, 63, 64, 65
vocabulary, 5, 21, 24, 31, 47, 48, 56, 64, 66, 77, 131, 134
working memory, 37, 81, 88
writing, 7, 46, 50, 55, 69, 74, 75, 88, 89, 90, 92, 96, 101, 102, 104, 105, 110, 111, 113, 114, 116, 119, 120, 130, 133, 134

written corrective feedback/WCF, 89, 90, 92, 93, 111, 114, 115, 116, 117, 119

Zone of Proximal Development, 115

www.ingramcontent.com/pod-product-compliance
Lightning Source LLC
Chambersburg PA
CBHW072053110526
44590CB00018B/3148